W. E. B. Du Bois

W. E. B. Du Bois

Pioneer American Sociologist

Robert A. Wortham

LEXINGTON BOOKS
Lanham • Boulder • New York • London

Rowman & Littlefield
Bloomsbury Publishing Inc, 1359 Broadway, New York, NY 10018, USA
Bloomsbury Publishing Plc, 50 Bedford Square, London, WC1B 3DP, UK
Bloomsbury Publishing Ireland, 29 Earlsfort Terrace, Dublin 2, D02 AY28, Ireland
www.bloomsbury.com

Published by Lexington Books
An imprint of The Rowman & Littlefield Publishing Group, Inc.
4501 Forbes Boulevard, Suite 200, Lanham, Maryland 20706
www.rowman.com

86-90 Paul Street, London EC2A 4NE

British Library Cataloguing in Publication Information available

Library of Congress Cataloging-in-Publication Data

Names: Wortham, Robert (Robert A.), author.
Title: W.E.B. Du Bois : pioneer American sociologist / Robert A. Wortham.
Description: Lanham : Lexington Books, [2022] | Includes bibliographical
    references and index.
Identifiers: LCCN 2022036953 (print) | LCCN 2022036954 (ebook) |
    ISBN 9781793610409 (cloth ; alk. paper) | ISBN 9781793610416 (ebook)
Subjects: LCSH: Du Bois, W. E. B. (William Edward Burghardt),
    1868–1963. | African American sociologists. | African Americans–Social
conditions—19th century. | African Americans—Social conditions—20th century. |
    Sociology—United States—History.
Classification: LCC E185.97.D73 W67 2022 (print) |
    LCC E185.97.D73 (ebook) | DDC 323.092 [B]—dc23/eng/20220826
LC record available at https://lccn.loc.gov/2022036953
LC ebook record available at https://lccn.loc.gov/2022036954

To all the NCCU Sociology graduate students who were part of the Du Bois seminar over the years.

Contents

List of Tables

Introduction

W. E. B. Du Bois: Pioneer American Sociologist

The period between 1890 and 1910 is a critical period in the development of sociology as a discipline in the United States. The diversity of voices in this period is reflected in the work of Anna Julia Cooper, Jane Addams, Carroll D. Wright, and Albion Woodbury Small. Cooper, an African American educator, activist, and sociologist from the South, conceptualized the intersection of race, gender, and social status within the South in her 1892 work, *A Voice from the South*. Jane Addams (1895) and others associated with the "Settlement Movement" produced community-based quality of life studies. Addams' work in Chicago was showcased in the 1895 publication *Hull-House Maps and Papers*. Carroll Wright, an applied sociologist and a statistician for the U.S. Commissioner of Labor, published a comprehensive study on practical, applied sociology titled *Outline of Practical Sociology* (1900). Albion Small was best known for his contributions to the development of the sociology program at the University of Chicago. An emphasis on community studies was a hallmark of the "Chicago School," and in 1894 Small partnered with George Vincent to produce an early sociology textbook, *An Introduction to Study of Society*. On the other hand, W. E. B. Du Bois, at Atlanta University, was conducting extensive, empirically based social studies on "the Negro problems" utilizing a triangular methodological approach to explore structural and cultural factors that were impacting African American quality of life and racial inequality in the United States.

This book, *W. E. B. Du Bois: Pioneer American Sociologist*, documents the massive volume of sociological work Du Bois generated during his first tenure at Atlanta University from 1897 through 1910. This sociological work showcases his pioneering impact on classical developments in the field in the United States and internationally. Leveraging the resources of the Atlanta

Sociological Laboratory, the annual Atlanta University Conferences, and the Atlanta University Press, Du Bois was able to plan, implement, and disseminate fact-based findings concerning "the Negro problems." Many of his seminal, early contributions to the discipline are presented in the following eight chapters.

The broad scope of his early sociological work is highlighted in chapter 1. Du Bois' theoretical and empirical, mixed-methods approaches to the study of sociological phenomena are presented in chapter 2. Furthermore, the groundbreaking work of the Atlanta Sociological Laboratory was routinely featured in the annual Atlanta University Conference annual reports that were published during Du Bois' first tenure at Atlanta University. The findings from two of these annual conferences on the scientific study of "the Negro Problems" (i.e., crime and health disparities) are discussed in chapter 2 as well. In chapter 3 the reader is introduced to Du Bois' early explorations in demography and urban sociology via his classic 1899 urban sociological investigation, *The Philadelphia Negro*. Du Bois' best-known rural social study on African American quality of life is the Farmville, Virginia study, which is summarized in chapter 4. Chapter 5 is devoted to a detailed discussion of Du Bois' unpublished Lowndes County, Alabama social study, which marked a turning point in the focus of his sociological career. Going forward, his primary emphasis rapidly turned from empirical sociology toward public sociology.

A comprehensive analysis of the Atlanta Black Church is provided in chapter 6. This case study is an example of Du Bois' pioneering work in the sociology of religion and the sociology of the Black Church. This chapter highlights the Atlanta Black Church religious economy and provides an early example of what is now known as "congregational analysis." Church leadership and children's religiosity are discussed also. In chapter 7 the reader is provided with an opportunity to experience how Du Bois was able to utilize prayers offered to Atlanta University students as a venue to provide social commentary on the African American experience at the beginning of the twentieth century. Du Bois' sociological legacy is showcased in chapter 8, where his pioneering, lasting contributions to the sociological perspective; to demography, urban, and rural sociology; and to religion and society are shared. Welcome to this journey through the extensive sociological investigations of one of the key figures in the development of sociology in the United States and globally.

CHAPTER 1

Du Bois and the Atlanta Sociological Tradition, 1897–1910

W. E. B. Du Bois generated a massive body of sociological work during his first tenure at Atlanta University from 1897 through 1910.[1] His contributions to the emerging discipline are seen in such areas as the scientific study of social problems, sociology for the general reader, the Southern Black Belt, and the Black Church and religion. Du Bois was a pioneer of American sociology and a classical figure associated with the development of the discipline globally. During his first tenure at Atlanta University, one witnesses the work of a prolific empirical sociologist while also observing his laying the foundation for a branch of sociology that what would later be known as public sociology.

THE STUDY OF SOCIAL PROBLEMS

Du Bois came to Atlanta University in July 1897 as a professor of history and economics (D. Lewis, 2009). Here he would develop further the work of the Atlanta Sociological Laboratory and continue the annual meetings of the Atlanta University Conferences on the Study of the Negro Problems. Although he left Atlanta University in July 1910 to assume the editorship of the NAACP's *The Crisis*, he established Atlanta University's reputation as what some sociologists believe to be the first School of Sociology (Morris, 2015; Wright II, 2016; Green and Wortham, 2015, 2018). His empirical approach to sociology, grounded in data-driven findings and addressing policy matters related to racial inequality and quality of life, characterized his approach to the study of sociology generally and of social problems specifically. A summary of the scope of Du Bois' pioneering work on the scientific study of social problems is presented in Table 1.1.

Table 1.1.   W. E. B. Du Bois and the Study of Social Problems: Pioneering Studies, 1897–1910

I. Perspectives on the Study of Social Problems
1. A program for a sociological society, 1897. Unpublished speech; W. E. B. Du Bois Papers (MS 312). Special Collections and University Archives, University of Massachusetts Amherst Libraries.
2. The study of the Negro problems. *Annals of the American Academy of Political and Social Science*, 11, (1898), 1–23.
3. *The Philadelphia Negro: a social study*. Philadelphia: University of Pennsylvania Press, 1899. Reprinted with an introduction by E. Anderson. Philadelphia: University of Pennsylvania Press, 1996.
4. Post graduate work in sociology in Atlanta University, 1900. Unpublished speech; W. E. B. Du Bois Papers (MS 312). Special Collections and University Archives, University of Massachusetts Amherst Libraries.
5. The Atlanta University conferences. *Charities*, 10, (1903), 435–439.

II. Atlanta University Conferences for the Study of the Negro Problems, 1898–1910
All studies were edited by W. E. B. Du Bois unless noted and were published in Atlanta by the Atlanta University Press.

First Cycle Studies
6. *Some efforts of American Negroes for their own social betterment*, 1898.
7. *The Negro in Business*, 1899.
8. *The College–bred Negro, 1900.*
9. *The Negro common school*, 1901.
10. *The Negro artisan*, 1902.
11. *The Negro church*, 1903. Reprinted with an introduction by P. Zuckerman, S. Barnes, and D. Cady. Walnut Creek, CA: AltaMira Press, 2003.
12. *Some notes on Negro crime particularly in Georgia*, 1904.
13. *A select bibliography of the American Negro*, 1905.

Second Cycle Studies
14. *The health and physique of the Negro American*, 1906.
15. *Economic co-operation among Negro Americans*, 1907.
16. *The Negro American family*, 1908; report copyright 1909. Reprinted as a facsimile edition. Santa Barbara, CA: Praeger, 1970.
17. *Efforts for social betterment among Negro Americans*, 1909; report copyright 1910.
18. *The College–bred Negro American*, 1910; report copyright 1911.[1]

---

1. This conference study was the first study to be co-edited by Augustus Dill. After formally leaving Atlanta University in July 1910, Du Bois and Dill would co-edit volumes addressing the common school (1911/12), artisans (1912/13), and morals and manners (1913/14). In his 1968 autobiography, published posthumously, Du Bois (1968/2007) indicated that projected conference studies after 1913 would address two new topics: 1) law and government and 2) literature and art.

Du Bois provided a preliminary vision statement of the role a program of sociology and a sociological club would play at Atlanta University in an unpublished 1897 address, "A Program for a Sociological Society." Here he delineated the scope of the discipline, noted how the study of society was grounded in the scientific method and specified how this methodological approach impacted data collection and analysis. Not restricting the primary focus of sociology to data collection and analysis, he was concerned also with how information obtained through empirical research could be utilized best. Forging ahead, Du Bois asked the sociological society to transition from simply discussing topics concerning African American quality of life to intentionally committing to collect empirical data that would paint a more accurate picture of the actual living conditions experienced by members of the African American community. Thinking within a clearinghouse context, Du Bois envisioned that the data collected could be utilized further by others. Atlanta University, through the work of the sociological club, the sociological laboratory, and the annual Atlanta University Conferences, could collaborate with other agencies committed to addressing empirically verified needs and could play a significant role in identifying issues demanding further investigation.

Du Bois provided a framework for studying social problems in his 1898 essay, "The Study of the Negro Problems." A social problem was conceptualized as a group's inability to actualize its desired ideals given the restriction in the range of specific courses of action available to its members within a given social setting. Since environmental conditions and available courses of action are fluid rather than static, Du Bois maintained that an integrated, interdisciplinary approach must be employed to adequately approach the study of racial inequality. For example, one could study African American employment by first providing a historical overview of African American employment, followed by the collection and analysis of available past and current statistical data on African American employment. This would be followed by an analysis of cultural and structural factors impacting African American employment within local and global contexts. Thus, the study of "the Negro problems" should integrate historical study, statistical investigation, anthropological measurement, and sociological interpretation (Du Bois, 1898a).

Du Bois' methodological approach to the study of social phenomena is exhibited in *The Philadelphia Negro* (1899a/1996) and in the Atlanta University Conference annual reports from 1898 through 1910. *The Philadelphia Negro* is a groundbreaking text in urban sociology, the study of social problems, and sociological research methods. Utilizing historical records, census and survey data, and qualitative data, Du Bois provided a comprehensive overview of African American life in Philadelphia generally and the

Seventh Ward specifically. The employment of a triangular methodology became the standard for his empirical approach to sociological investigation and enabled him to become a pioneer in the development of scientific sociology. In this massive study, Du Bois addressed demographic issues (e.g., migration and population composition), African American organizational life (e.g., churches and benevolence societies), and social issues (e.g., racial inequality, class differences, prejudice, and voting rights). Many of the issues noted here are addressed in more depth in the annual Atlanta University Conferences.

From 1898 to 1909, Du Bois edited twelve conference reports and co-edited the 1910 report with Augustus Dill (Table 1.1). All reports were published by the Atlanta University Press. Each annual conference was designed to address an important social issue faced by the African American community. The cycle of topics was to be repeated every ten years to provide a baseline, whereby changes in the quality of life of the African American community, particularly in the South, could be gauged (Du Bois, 1903a). Du Bois assumed the role as editor of the annual conference reports with the third study in the first cycle. The reports generally discussed the scope of the annual inquiry, provided a discussion of any survey instrument employed, and presented the results of the survey findings and any other studies that had been conducted that were relevant to the topic under consideration. The studies concluded with a summary discussion of the investigation's major findings, and the adopted resolutions were stated. The reports were known throughout the United States and globally and were examples of empirical research that advanced the development of scientific sociology well before a formal textbook on the topic, *Introduction to the Science of Sociology*, was published by E. W. Burgess and Robert Park in 1921.

SOCIOLOGY FOR PUBLIC CONSUMPTION

By 1903, Du Bois was able to demonstrate that his sociological endeavors could appeal to the general reader. His best-known book, *The Souls of Black Folk* (1903b/2007), was originally proposed as a work to showcase several of his article-length studies on "the Negro problems," which had been published between 1897 and 1902. However, the Chicago publisher, A. C. McClurg, wanted Du Bois to consider providing a study that would appeal more to a general readership. Du Bois responded by slightly revising eight previously published articles and adding five new essays. Table 1.2 provides a breakdown of the previously published revised essays and the new essays.

In the revised essays, Du Bois addressed such topics as racial identity, racial inequality, racial interaction, the economic transformation of the South, the development of African American leadership, and rural life in the Southern Black Belt as well as education, crime, and the role of the Black Church in the African American experience. Appealing to the general reader, the revised and newly added essays offered Du Bois an opportunity to provide a more racially and ethnically diverse audience with a glimpse of how "the color line" impacted African American quality of life. Readers were able to experience what "life within the Veil" entailed, what it was like to be characterized as "a problem," what the leadership role of "the Talented Tenth" would entail, and how to understand the reality that

Table 1.2.   Social Problems and the Popular Audience: W. E. B. Du Bois' *The Souls of Black Folk,* **1903**

The souls of Black folk. A. C. McClurg, 1903. Reprint edited by H. Gates, Jr., with an introduction by A. Rampersad. New York: Oxford University Press, 2007. The volume included thirteen essays as well as a "forethought" and an "afterthought."

I. Previously Published Revised Essays, 1897–1902
1. Strivings of the Negro people. *The Atlantic Monthly*, 80, (1897), 194–198. Reprinted as chapter 1, Of our spiritual strivings.
2. A Negro schoolmaster in the new South. *The Atlantic Monthly*, 83, (1899), 99–105. Reprinted as chapter 4, Of the meaning of progress.
3. The religion of the American Negro. *New World*, 9, (1900), 614–625. Reprinted as chapter 10, Of the faith of the fathers.
4. The Freedman's Bureau. *The Atlantic Monthly*, 87, (1901), 354–365. Reprinted as chapter 2, Of the dawn of freedom.
5. The Negro as he really is. *The World's Work*, 2, (1901), 846–866. Reprinted as chapter 7, of the Black Belt and chapter 8, Of the quest of the golden fleece.
6. The evolution of Negro leadership. *The Dial*, 31, (1901), 53–55. Reprinted as chapter 3, Of Mr. Booker T. Washington and others.
7. The relation of the Negroes to the whites in the South. *Annals of the American Academy of Political and Social Science*, 18, (1901), 121–140. Reprinted as chapter 9, Of the sons of master and man.
8. Of the training of black men. *The Atlantic Monthly*, 90, (1902), 289–297. Reprinted as chapter 6, Of the training of black men.

II. New Essays
9. Chapter 5, Of the wings of Atalanta.
10. Chapter 11, Of the passing of the first-born.
11. Chapter 12, Of Alexander Crummell.
12. Chapter 13, Of the coming of John.
13. Chapter 14, The sorrow songs.

African American identity in the United States was an expression of "double consciousness." The leadership role of the "Talented Tenth" was specified further in another writing from 1903 (Du Bois, 1903c).

With the five newly added essays, Du Bois demonstrated how the arts and humanities could provide richer contextual venues for more comprehensive sociological portraits of a group's lived experiences. In the first new essay, "Of the Wings of Atalanta," the story of the female huntress from Greek mythology, Atalanta, provided Du Bois with a platform for documenting Atlanta's decline as the queen of the cotton kingdom and the city's increasing industrialization. Next, autobiography provided Du Bois with a venue to discuss the death of his first child in one of his most personal essays, "Of the Passing of the First-Born." Du Bois described how racial prejudice and discrimination experienced personally within a segregated health care environment had tragically impacted his life. In "Of Alexander Crummell," Du Bois demonstrated how biography provided an effective format to showcase the strengths and vision of an African American religious leader and once again allowed Du Bois to show readers how prejudice and discrimination created an uneven playing field throughout American society and within Crummell's chosen profession. Employing the short-story format in "Of the Coming of John," Du Bois shared a story of a childhood interracial friendship that could not be maintained in adulthood, thus highlighting how the "norms" governing racial interaction varied with environmental context. Delving into the power of music and lyrics to capture the African American community's experience of slavery, Du Bois concluded *The Souls of Black Folk* with an essay on the "sorrow songs."

This brief review of the studies on "the Negro problems" presented in the first two tables documents how Du Bois appropriated the social study and popular formats to convey his empirically observed findings. While many of the studies focused on urban or rural areas, several of his additional studies addressed everyday life within a particular region—the Southern Black Belt.

SOUTHERN BLACK BELT

In *The Southern Black Belt: A National Perspective* (1997), Ronald Wimberley and Libby Morris provide an assessment of the quality of life in the Southern Black Belt based on a county-level analysis of 1990 census data. The study specifically addresses socioeconomic conditions in counties with an African American population of 12 percent or more throughout the Southeast (i.e., Virginia through Texas) and reveals that poverty; low educational attainment; unemployment; and total, youth, and elder dependence correlate with the percent of the population who are African American. While this study has become a definitive study on the region at the end of the twentieth century, its empirical findings echo those documented by W. E. B. Du. Bois in a series of sociological studies of the Southern Black Belt at the end of the nineteenth century and the beginning of the twentieth. These pioneering studies are listed in Table 1.3.

Between 1897 and 1904, the U.S. Bureau of Labor published nine studies on African American quality of life in the United States (Grossman, 1974), and four of these empirically based studies were conducted by Du Bois and addressed the living conditions of African Americans in the rural South. The

Table 1.3. W. E. B. Du Bois and the Southern Black Belt: Selected Empirically Based Studies, 1898–1909

I. Department of Labor Studies, 1898–1904
1. The Negroes of Farmville, Virginia: a social study. U.S. Department of Labor. *Bulletin*, 3, no. 14, (1898), 1–38.
2. The Negro in the Black Belt: some social sketches. U.S. Department of Labor. *Bulletin*, 4, no. 22, (1899), 401–417.
3. The Negro landholder of Georgia. U.S. Department of Labor. *Bulletin*, 6, no. 35, (1901), 647–777.
4. The Negro farmer. U.S. Department of Labor. *Bulletin*, 8, (1904), 69–98.[1]

Additional Studies, 1900–1909
5. The Georgia Negro: a social study. Paris Exposition (*Exposition Universelle),* April 15–November 12, 1900. The Negro Exhibit.[2]
6. Die Negerfrage in den Vereinigten Staaten. *Socialpolitik*, 22, (1906), 21–79. This study was translated by Joseph Fracchia and published as The Negro question in the United States. *The new centennial review*, 6, (2006), 241–290.
7. Negro labor in Lowndes County, Alabama. This unpublished study is based on survey research findings.[3]

1. An expanded edition of this study was republished in 1906. The expanded edition included 38 new statistical tables created by W. C. Hunt and W. F. Wilcox. No additional narrative was added by Du Bois. The expanded edition was released by the United States Department of Commerce and Labor. Bureau of the Census as *Special reports: supplementary analysis and derivative tables. Twelfth census of the United States, 1900,* Part 2 (511–579). The report was published by the Government Printing Office.

2. This study was published in 2018 as *W. E. B. Du Bois's data portraits visualizing Black America: the color line at the turn of the twentieth century,* W. Battle-Baptiste and B. Russert, (Eds.). New York: Princeton Architectural Press.

3. On November 9, 1908, Commissioner Neill informed Du Bois that the study was to be published in the January 1909 issue of the Department's *Bulletin* (Du Bois, 1908d). W. E. B. Du Bois Papers (MS 312). Special Collections and University Archives, University of Massachusetts Amherst Libraries.

1898 study was a small area social study based on a survey that allowed Du Bois to provide a comprehensive study of African American quality of life in Farmville, Virginia. Topics covered included population growth, real estate, marital status and family size, educational attainment, occupations, income, housing, and religious life. Du Bois relied on the work of students and practitioners to create brief social sketches in the 1899 study of African American quality life in six areas of varying size in Georgia and Alabama. For each location, data were collected on African American family size. While the number of variables covered in the surveys varied by location, other data collected included the African American age-sex distribution, wages and/or family income, marital status, occupation, and home ownership.

In the 1901 study, "The Negro Landholder of Georgia," Du Bois presented and discussed state- and county-level data on African American land ownership, farm size, and property values. Some of these data were provided also at the town-city level. Additionally, the report discussed the growth of the African American population in Georgia since 1790, the rise of the crop lien (metayer) system, and African American ownership of farm equipment and household goods.

A description of Bibb County in central Georgia is provided as an example of the type data Du Bois summarized at the county level. The reader was informed that the county was established in 1822, the soil quality varied from good to poor, and in 1890 the population of the city of Macon was 22,746 persons. Macon's African American population at the time was 11,203 (i.e., 49.3 percent of the total). For the county as a whole, the white population outnumbered the African American population from 1830 to 1860, but the pattern reversed for 1870−1890. Finally, from 1875 to 1900, the total assessed value of African American–owned land in Bibb County increased from $253,159 to $683,990. Du Bois viewed landownership as a key indicator of social mobility.

The last empirical study by Du Bois published by the Bureau of Labor was the 1904 study, "The Negro Farmer." It was republished in 1906 with expanded statistical material provided by the Census Bureau. In this report Du Bois (1904a) compared African American farmers who owned their own farms to African American tenant farmers operating farms under the crop lien system. The report began with a comprehensive discussion of African American–owned farms, and the issues addressed included number of farms owned, acreage, property value of the farm (i.e., land, buildings, and equipment), farm income generated, and finally expenses associated with labor and fertilizer. Detailed discussions on these topics were provided collectively and by geographic region and by states. Shifting the focus to factors impacting African American tenant farmers, Du Bois demonstrated how these farmers had been impacted by slavery and the crop lien system.

The last two sections of the report highlighted the important role African American farmers played in the development of American agriculture generally and throughout the Southern Black Belt. Du Bois noted that African American farmers were producing 40 percent of the cotton, 20 percent of the sweet potatoes, 10 percent of the tobacco, and 10 percent of the rice in the United States. Most of this production came from African American farmers in the South. Furthermore, in a significant number of counties within the Southern Black Belt in 1900, three hundred or more of the farms in the county were owned by African Americans (Du Bois, 1904a).

Three additional empirically based studies on the quality of life of African Americans residing in the Southern Black Belt were conducted by Du Bois between 1900 and 1909. The first study, "The Georgia Negro: A Social Study," included a series of sixty-three maps, graphs, and plates that were not published during Du Bois' lifetime but were part of the Negro Exhibit at the 1900 Paris Exhibition (*Exposition Universelle*). Color plate versions of these sixty-three visual data images along with contextual essays by contemporary researchers were published in 2018 in a volume edited by Battle-Baptiste and Russert. On the title page of the exhibit study, Du Bois provided one of the earliest statements of his well-known expression, "The problem of the 20th century is the problem of the color-line." The exhibit provided summary demographic data on the African American population in the United States and in the state of Georgia at the beginning of the twentieth century (Du Bois, 1900a).

The Georgia plates displayed data on such demographic characteristics as African American migration, marital status, and illiteracy as well as social and economic characteristics like school enrollment, teachers in public schools, land ownership and land value, occupations and income, and family budgets. Maps were utilized to document the geographic distribution of the African American population in selected areas. The remaining plates featured data of the African American population for the country as a whole and showcased data on the distribution and growth of the African American population throughout the United States. These data addressed such topics as occupations, teachers, illiteracy, school enrollment, slavery, rural and urban population in the South, marital status, land ownership, business involvement, poverty, mortality, crime, published news outlets, and religion (Du Bois, 1900a). Collectively, these sixty-three plates documented the quality of life of the African American community in the United States and Georgia at the turn of the twentieth century in addition to providing a visual benchmark, whereby future improvements or lack thereof could be assessed.

In 1906, at the request of Max Weber, Du Bois published a general study about "the Negro Problems" in the United States. The study was published in the *Archiv fur Sozialwissenschaft und Sozialpolitik*, a journal co-edited by Weber. The study, "Die Negerfrage in den Vereinigten Staaten" (The Negro Question in the United States), did not appear in English translation until 2006 when Joseph Fracchia's translation was featured in the journal *New Centennial Review* (volume 6, issue 3).

Du Bois began the study by summarizing the impact of the legacy of slavery and the plantation system on the nature and degree of economic development within the African American community in the South. Attention turned next to a discussion of the decline of the large plantation system and the rise of the sharecropping and crop lien system throughout the South. Under these systems, freed slaves worked a plot of land, but varying portions of the monies received from the crops' yield were taken first to pay for the workers' use of tools, animals, and provisions needed by the worker and additional family members. Under these systems of operation, workers were often in debt. With the dismantling of large farms following the Civil War, average farm size in the South declined from 335.4 acres in 1860 to 138.2 acres in 1900 (Du Bois, 1906a/2006). Du Bois then reminded the reader that cotton was the main currency utilized throughout the South and that a farmer's success and failure were pegged to the price of cotton.

Next, Du Bois discussed the growth of the African American population in the United States from 1750 to 1900 and documented the increase in African American literacy from 1860 to 1900. Data provided revealed that one-third (33.7 percent) of African American workers were employed in agriculture, which was the largest employment category. Turning to a discussion of African American farms in 1900, data on African American farm property owners versus renters/sharecroppers for all the states comprising the Southern Black Belt as well as a few adjacent states and territories were provided. The percentage of African American property owners exceeded renters and sharecroppers in West Virginia, Oklahoma, Virginia, Maryland, and the Indian Territory. However, in several of the "Deep South" states (i.e., South Carolina, Mississippi, Louisiana, Alabama, and Georgia), the percentage of African American farms run by African American property owners varied from 13.7 percent in Georgia to 22.2 percent in South Carolina (Du Bois, 1906a/2006).

Du Bois concluded this 1906 study by discussing the impact of segregation on quality of life in the South. Particular areas of racial interaction highlighted included cultural life, economic opportunities, voting rights, taxation, and patterns of social interaction. Du Bois underscored the fact that the color line and inequality were specifically linked in a race-based caste system. The study concluded with an appeal for continued improvements in the African American community's quest for human rights and justice.

Finally, a social study on Lowndes County, Alabama was envisioned as early as 1902 (Du Bois, 1902a), and a comprehensive study on African American labor in Lowndes County was conducted from 1906 to early 1908. The study was sponsored by the U.S. Bureau of Labor and was based on a 1906 survey. Du Bois was assisted with data collection by sociologists Monroe Work and Richard R. Wright, Jr., as well as by John Lemon, a staff member of the Calhoun Colored School in Lowndes County. This study would have been Du Bois' largest, most extensive empirical rural study. A final report was submitted; Du Bois was paid for his efforts, and the final report was to be published in the January 1909 issue of the *Bulletin of the Department of Labor* (Du Bois, 1908d). This study was Du Bois' last major attempt to provide an academic empirical study on "the Negro problems." Unfortunately, it was never published.

SOCIOLOGY OF RELIGION

W. E. B. Du Bois is the founding figure of the sociological study of the Black Church and a pioneer in the sociology of religion (Wortham, 2005a, 2009a, 2018a). He blended an empirical approach to the study of religion with his commitment to specify and understand how historical, social, and cultural contexts impacted religious experiences and institutions. These aims underscored his unwavering commitment to provide empirically based observations and facts in his quest for "truth" (Du Bois, 1899a/1996). Du Bois' early sociological studies of the Black Church laid the foundation for further sociologically based research on the Black Church by Benjamin Mays and Joseph Nicholson (*The Negro's Church*, 1933), E. Franklin Frazier (*The*

Negro Church in America, 1964), C. Eric Lincoln and Lawrence H. Mamiya (*The Black Church in the African American Experience*, 1991), Andrew Billingsley (*Mighty Like a River: The Black Church and Social Reform*, 1999), Omar McRoberts (*Streets of Glory: Church and Community in a Black Urban Neighborhood*, 2003), Walter Earl Fluker (*The Ground Has Shifted: The Future of the Black Church in Post-Racial America*, 2016), and Henry Louis Gates, Jr. (*The Black Church: This Is Our Story, This Is Our Song*, 2021). A list of Du Bois' pioneering works in the sociology of the Black Church and the sociology of religion is presented in Table 1.4.

His discussion of the six functions of Philadelphia's Black Church in *The Philadelphia Negro* (1899a/1996) represented an early "functional analysis" of a religious group. Du Bois' proposed framework addressed finances, membership, social activities, moral standards, the provision of educational opportunities, and the promotion of social reform and change. In *The Negro Church* (1903c/2003), an Atlanta University Conference report, Du Bois provided the earliest book-length example of an empirical study of a religious group by a sociologist. Utilizing a triangular methodological approach, he integrated the findings from religious census data, denominational statistics, small area surveys, ethnographic fieldwork, and historical studies to portray the vibrant role the Black Church played in the African American community at the end of the nineteenth century and the beginning of the twentieth.

In three essays included in *The Souls of Black Folk* (1903b/2007), Du Bois discussed the central, integrative roles the Black Church, church leadership, and religious music played within the African American experience in the United States. The specific essays are: "Of the Faith of the Fathers," which addressed the role of the church in the community, "Alexander Crummell," which focused on church leadership opportunities, and "The Sorrow Songs," which showcased traditional music's power to capture the essence of lived experiences.

In other sociological essays and book chapters published between 1897 and 1907, Du Bois commented on how the Black Church could impact the African American community in a positive manner through its sponsorship of social gatherings (Du Bois, 1897b) and by functioning as the center of religious and organizational life in small rural communities like Farmville, Virginia (Du Bois, 1898b), and large cities like Philadelphia (Du Bois, 1899a/1996). In two additional essays from this period, Du Bois provided extensive discussions of the role the Black Church played in the social,

Table 1.4.   W. E. B. Du Bois and the Sociology of Religion: Pioneering Studies, 1897–1910[1]

1. The problem of amusement. *The Southern Workman*, 27, (1897), 181–184
2. The Negroes of Farmville, Virginia: a social study. U.S. Department of Labor. *Bulletin*, 3, no. 14, (1898), 1–38. Pages 34–38 contain a discussion of the Black churches in Farmville.
3. The church. In *Some efforts of American Negroes for their own social betterment* (Section 3, pages 5–12). Atlanta: Atlanta University Press, 1898.
4. The organized life of Negroes. In *The Philadelphia Negro: a social study*. Philadelphia: University of Pennsylvania Press, 1899. Reprinted with an introduction by E. Anderson. Philadelphia: University of Pennsylvania Press, 1996. (Sections 31–33, pages 197–221).
5. The religion of the American Negro. *New World* 9, (1900), 614–625. This essay was later published in *The souls of Black folk*. Chicago: A. C. McClurg, 1903, as Of the faith of the fathers. Reprint in *The souls of Black folk*, edited by H. L. Gates, Jr., and introduction by A. Rampersad (90–98). New York: Oxford University Press, 2007.
6. Of Alexander Crummell. In *The souls of Black folk*. Chicago: A. C. McClurg, 1903. Reprint *The souls of Black folk*, edited by H. Gates, Jr. and introduction by A. Rampersad (103–109). New York: Oxford University Press, 2007.
7. The sorrow songs. In *The souls of Black folk*. Chicago: A. C. McClurg, 1903. Reprint *The souls of Black folk*, edited by H. L. Gates, Jr., and introduction by A. Rampersad (121–129). New York: Oxford University Press, 2007.
8. *The Negro church*. Atlanta: Atlanta University Press, 1903. Reprint with an introduction by P. Zuckerman, S. Barnes, and D. Cady. Walnut Creek, CA: AltaMira Press, 2003.
9. The development of a people. *International Journal of Ethics*, 14, (1904), 292–311.
10. Credo. *The Independent*, 57, (1904), 787.
11. A litany at Atlanta. *The Independent*, 61, (1906), 856–858.
12. The church. In *Economic co-operation among Negro Americans* (Section 9, pages 54–73). Atlanta: Atlanta University Press, 1907.
13. Religion in the South. In B. T. Washington and W. E. B. Du Bois, *The Negro in the South* (125–191, 214–222). Philadelphia: George W. Jacobs, 1907. This is the fourth and concluding essay in the volume.
14. The church. In *Efforts for social betterment among Negro Americans* (Section 5, pages 16–29). Atlanta: Atlanta University Press, 1909.
15. *Prayers for dark people*, H. Aptheker (Ed.) and introduction by H. Aptheker. Amherst: University of Massachusetts Press (1980). Du Bois composed these prayers for Atlanta University students around 1909–1910, but they were not published until 1980.

---

1. The writings listed below are included completely or partially in R. Wortham (Ed.). *W. E. B. Du Bois and the sociology of the Black church and religion, 1897–1914*. Lanham, MD: Lexington Books, 2018.

economic, and spiritual development of the African American community throughout the South from the period of slavery to the present (Du Bois, 1904b, 1907a). Furthermore, the Black Church's contributions to "social betterment and economic cooperation" within the African American community were assessed in the Atlanta University Conference reports of 1898, 1907, and 1909 (Tables 1.1 and 1.4). Once again switching genres, Du Bois' views on the potential power and influence of the Black Church and religion on African American lived experience were expressed in two of his early poetic works, "Credo" (Du Bois, 1904c) and "A Litany at Atlanta" (Du Bois, 1906b), as well as through prayers written for Atlanta University students. These prayers appear to have been written between 1909 and 1910 but were not published until 1980 in the volume *Prayers for Dark People*.

For Du Bois, these prayers became a vehicle that allowed him to help impressionable children and young adults: 1) understand their experience of double consciousness; 2) become aware of the social issues that were impacting African Americans' quality of life; 3) realize why emerging leaders would need to be persons of strong character; and 4) paint a vision of racial equality that challenged the plausibility of existing social structures. Since Du Bois left Atlanta University in July 1910 to assume the position of publications director at the NAACP, these prayers come from the final phase of his early sociological period and help document his transition from an inductive, empirical sociologist interested in presenting facts that would provide a basis for social reform to an impassioned social activist committed to the promotion and achievement of social justice.

NOTE

1. Some of the material included in this chapter is based on material that was published previously as "Introduction to the Sociology of W. E. B. Du Bois," *Sociation Today* 3.1 (2005), www.ncsociology.org/sociationtoday. The material incorporated in this chapter has been revised, and permission to include the revised, previously published material has been obtained from the editor of *Sociation Today*.

CHAPTER 2

Pioneering Efforts in the Development of Scientific Sociology

During sociology's early formative period in the United States, many of the early sociological thinkers, like Lester Ward (1883), William Graham Sumner (1906), and Franklin Giddings (1896), were primarily formulating and utilizing theoretical constructs to study the nature of society.[1] W. E. B. Du Bois was more concerned with framing sociology as a science whereby human behavior could be observed and measured empirically and where the differing impacts of social structures on the quality of life of persons engaging in these structures could be assessed. Just as the scientific method could be applied to the natural sciences, Du Bois believed this method could be extended to the social and behavioral sciences.

Thus, while Albion Small and other researchers affiliated with the University of Chicago were conducting small area sociological studies, at Atlanta University, W. E. B. Du Bois was conducting extensive, empirically based social studies on "the Negro problems" utilizing a triangular methodological approach. He understood that theory and research were key components of scientific inquiry. This was illustrated clearly in his 1905 essay, "Sociology Hesitant."

THE SCOPE OF SOCIOLOGY

Before turning to a discussion of "Sociology Hesitant," one can see how much Du Bois' framing of sociology as a science provided a foundation for how sociology is taught, studied, and practiced today. Students attending their first sociology class discover that sociology is a social science grounded in the empirical method. The quest for social facts and the identification of forces that shape, transform, and preserve the social order are enhanced through scientific investigation. As students are encouraged to develop and utilize their "sociological imaginations" (Mills, 1959; Berger, 1963), they are often introduced to some variation on Wallace's (1971) "cycle of scientific inquiry." Theory, hypotheses, observations, and generalizations are cornerstones of the scientific method. Ways of conceptualizing the social order and social interaction patterns (i.e., theoretical paradigms) are introduced, and knowledge claims (i.e., hypotheses) are proposed and evaluated. Social phenomena (i.e., observations) are identified, measured, and analyzed, and at some point, summary findings (i.e., generalizations) are brought forward. These findings may be compared with previous findings, or they may open new venues prompting further study. Students begin to realize that sociology is not a list of topics that can be used to stimulate interesting, relevant discussion. Rather, sociology is a craft that is practiced. Thus, how did Du Bois define sociology's scope?

His early sociological work was not conducted in a theoretical vacuum. Auguste Comte approached the study of society from an evolutionary perspective and argued that societies were shaped by social forces promoting stability (i.e., social statics) and change (i.e., social dynamics) and over time, societies evolved from simple to more complex forms. Employing a functional approach to the study of society, Emile Durkheim maintained that society was a system of interdependent parts and that each part had a function or purpose. Society's norms and social structures functioned to promote equilibrium and stability. Addressing power structures within a society, Karl Marx argued that the organizations and groups that controlled or owned society's productive assets (i.e., the means of production) shaped society to reflect their own interests. Max Weber, also a conflict theorist, noted that status groups within a society, which were identified by such factors as race, age, gender, and social class, competed against each other for available power. Weber believed that power was regulated by a group's access to property, power, and prestige. Du Bois approached the study of society from an integrated, multidisciplinary perspective as he framed sociology as a science. This was articulated more intentionally in "Sociology Hesitant."

For Du Bois (1905a/2000) sociology's primary focus is the study of human actions. These actions could be observed and measured. Classical sociologists, like Comte and Herbert Spencer, had been content to study theoretical abstractions. Du Bois framed this distinction as follows:

Instead of seeking men as the natural unit of associated men, it strayed further in metaphysical lines, and confounding Things with Thoughts of Things, they sought not the real element of Society but the genesis of our social ideas. Society became for them a mode of mental action, and its germ was—according to their ingenuity—"Consciousness of Kind," "Imitation," the "Social Imperative," and the like. (Du Bois, 1905a/2000, 40)

Human actions can be observed; patterns could be documented; and laws could be formulated. However, since the range of choices for action among people can vary, human actions cannot be predicted with absolute certainty. Chance factors impact behavior. Human behavior can be influenced by culture, norms, and social structures. In this manner sociology is not an exact science like physics, but it is still an empirical science.

Du Bois (1905a/2000) asserted that scientific sociology is grounded in a fundamental paradox. Human action can be patterned and formulated as laws, but actions can also be random and subject to chance variation. Since humans can exercise free will, persons, to varying degrees, may modify their range of responses. Thus, the historical, social, and cultural contexts framing human behavior must be assessed empirically to the degree that it is possible to do so.

Groups are critical units of analysis in sociological investigations. This is one of the cornerstones of social research to which sociology students today are introduced in their beginning research classes. In studying human behavior in varying environmental contexts, Du Bois (1905a/2000, 43–44) insisted that a unified theory of science was needed, stating, "Some such reconciliation of the two great wings of science must come. It is inconceivable that the present dualism in classified knowledge can continue much longer. Mutual understanding must come under a working hypothesis which will give scope to Historian as well as Biologist." Scientific silos are therefore counterproductive. Some of the sciences are more exact than others, and, in the social and behavioral sciences, more room must be given to chance factors. Our statistical models today often distinguish explained and unexplained variation. This is particularly the case when studying human behavior in an uncontrolled, non-laboratory environment.

Thus, sociology is a science that seeks to observe and measure human behavior and specify patterns of human behavior (e.g., laws) while also taking into account the impact that chance factors (e.g., free will) play in attempting to describe behavior accurately. Thus, sociology's scope incorporated theory

and research methods as complementary and not mutually exclusive ele-
ments. Attention is now directed toward Du Bois' utilization of a triangular
methodological approach in his early sociological investigations.

INSTITUTIONALIZING METHODOLOGICAL TRIANGULATION

Students enrolled in basic sociology research methods classes are introduced
to concepts like types of variables, units of analysis, participant observation,
different types of samples, surveys and questionnaires, and the reliability and
validity of survey data (Babbie, 2016). Do our measures of social phenomena adequately describe the phenomena under investigation? Are our studies
based on representative samples? Can one measure be verified by another,
and what researcher biases have been introduced? These are basic research
concerns that students are trained to address. Students are exposed also to
different ways of gathering data and to various types of research design. A
basic distinction is usually made between experimental and non-experimental
research design. Typically, more attention is devoted to different examples
of non-experimental research design, like secondary analysis, surveys and
interviews, participant observation, and ethnographic description. Students
know that these techniques can be placed in their research toolbox, but how
often are they reminded that a better understanding of how social factors
interact may be obtained if more than one research method is employed?

Consider the following example of the utilization of a triangular methodology by Omar McRoberts (2003) in his study of the changing religious
marketplace in Boston's "Four Corners." This study of an African American
urban neighborhood is grounded in data obtained from four years of participant observation research, interviews with clergy, community development
leaders and residents, as well as archival data (e.g., census data and maps).
Based on an analysis of the twenty-nine congregations comprising the "Four
Corners" religious district, McRoberts concludes that religious groups primarily provide their members with the skills needed to: 1) be a presence in
an impoverished community; 2) serve as support groups for African American migrants from the South; and 3) enable immigrants to adapt to Boston's
urban environment through a process of more extensive assimilation. The
local neighborhood focus and the concern with racial and ethnic change
are reminiscent of the "social study" approach associated with Du Bois and
the Atlanta Sociological Laboratory and the "community study" approach

of Robert Park, Ernest Burgess, and Roderick McKenzie and the Chicago School. It is reflected also in the Wilson and Taub 2006 study on the racial, ethnic, and economic conditions of four Chicago neighborhoods.

In his sociological studies of urban and rural quality of life and in his studies of "the Negro Problems" in the different Atlanta University Conferences, Du Bois utilized a mixed-methods, triangular methodological approach. Routinely, he would investigate an issue involving some aspect of racial inequality, like wages and employment opportunities, by collecting historical data, utilizing available census data, and designing and implementing surveys. Also, when feasible, ethnographic data were collected. This provided Du Bois with a more comprehensive, empirical assessment of the issue under investigation. This triangular methodological approach was institutionalized by Du Bois and was his methodological trademark.

Du Bois was trained to work within an interdisciplinary perspective rather than operate within academic silos. During his doctoral studies in Berlin from 1892 to 1894, Du Bois encountered the work of Gustav Schmoller and was introduced to an interdisciplinary area of study known as *Staatswissenschaften* (i.e., the scientific study of the state; social politics). This program of study integrated insights from diverse academic fields like economics, history, political science, public administration, sociology, and statistics (Fischer, 1968). Schmoller introduced Du Bois to the inductive method and argued that social policy must be grounded in scientific, empirical facts. The researcher is to study "what is" rather than "what ought to be" (Boston, 1991; Broderick, 1958).

To illustrate Du Bois' use of methodological triangulation in the contextual study of "the Negro Problems," a closer look at an urban and a rural setting is provided. The urban example involves the discussion of the income of the residents in Philadelphia's Seventh Ward taken from Du Bois' classic 1899 study in urban sociology, *The Philadelphia Negro*.

A description of the class distinctions within Philadelphia's African American population is provided in the section on income (Du Bois, 1899a/1996). Since Du Bois expressed concern about the accuracy of the financial information obtained from the survey question addressing yearly family income, he provided reconstructed yearly income data based on estimates of weekly or monthly income, rent paid, wife's employment, rental income from lodgers, and his own projections. Based on this revised income tabulation method, 18.5 percent of families were classified as "very poor to poor," earning $5 a week or less; 47 percent of families were identified as "fair" and were earning $5–$9.99 weekly, and another 29.5 percent of families were classified as "comfortable to good," earning between $10 and $19.99 a week. The "well-to-do" families, who were earning $20 a week or more, comprised 4.2 percent of all families.

After specifying the income distribution of the Seventh Ward's African American residents, Du Bois provided a summary description of each social class and a few representative case studies from within each group. Ethnographic descriptions were used to complement and reinforce the general statistical patterns noted for each group. For example, Du Bois (1899a/1996) noted that slum residents typically resided in one- or two-room residences that were poorly heated. Paid employment and children's education were sporadic, and church attendance was low. Prostitution and crime were common.

One three-member family included in the "very poor" class was described in the following manner:

> Both the husband and the son are out of work. They live in one filthy room, twelve feet by fourteen, scantily furnished and poorly ventilated. The woman works at service and receives about three dollars a week. They pay twelve dollars a month for three rooms, and sub-rent two of them to other families, which makes their rent about three dollars a week. (Du Bois, 1899a/1996, 173)

With food running $1 a week and heating expenses averaging another $0.56 a week during the winter, virtually nothing was left for health care and unexpected expenses. This brief ethnographic account enabled Du Bois to move beyond cold statistical description to provide a more nuanced portrait of a family living in poverty. This is an example of the type of rich contextual data that can be obtained when utilizing a mixed-methods research design.

The rural example of Du Bois' utilization of a triangular research design is taken from his 1898 study of African American life in Farmville, Virginia. Quality of life data characterizing the African American residents of Farmville were obtained from a brief twenty-one item survey schedule, which included questions on occupation and income. Farmville's African American labor force data were based on the population over age 10, and the population was almost evenly divided among persons employed in domestic service (31.8 percent), as industrial laborers (30.5 percent), or unemployed (28.0 percent). The remaining tenth of the labor force was engaged in one of the professions, business, or agriculture. Domestic work was seen as a remnant of slavery and was not perceived favorably. Most industrial workers were employed in the preparation of tobacco strips, but this occupation did not provide year-round employment. Seasonal employment and irregular work were identified as major factors impacting household income and available employment opportunities (Du Bois, 1898b).

Turning to social class, Du Bois (1898b) placed families into one of four categories based on weekly to monthly wages. One in nine families (11.1 percent) were classified as living in poverty. Almost half (48.9 percent) the families were identified as working class, and another fourth (24.0 percent) were viewed as middle class. The upper class was sizable (16.0 percent of families).

The survey findings on family income and social class were complemented by ethnographic descriptions obtained via participant observation. Du Bois provided a "slice of life" of an affluent African American family as he recounted his experience at a dinner hosted by a Farmville grocer.

> The host was a young man in the thirties, with good common school training. There were eight in his family. . . . The house, a neat two-story frame, with 6 or 8 rooms, was on Main street, and was recently purchased of white people. . . . There was a flower and vegetable garden, cow and pigs, etc. The party consisted of a mail clerk and his wife; a barber's wife, the widowed daughter of the wood merchant; a young man, an employee in a tobacco factory, and his wife, who had been in service in Connecticut; a middle aged woman, graduate of Hampton, and others. After a preliminary chat, the company assembled in a back dining room. The host and hostess did not seat themselves, but served the company with chicken, ham, potatoes, corn, bread and butter, cake and ice cream. Afterwards the company went to the parlor and talked and sang— mostly hymns—by the aid of a little organ, which the widow played. (Du Bois, 1898b, 36)

Note the attention Du Bois gave to the details of the evening such as etiquette, the meal served, and entertainment. In describing the distinguishing characteristics of the host, the home, and the guests, he managed also to answer many of the quality of life questions included in the Farmville survey schedule. Du Bois' skill as a participant observer/ethnographer is demonstrated here, and once again, the rich contextual data provided by a triangular methodology are evident. Attention now turns to Du Bois' approach to sociology at Atlanta University and samples of the work generated for the annual Atlanta University Conferences.

SOCIOLOGY AT ATLANTA UNIVERSITY AND THE ATLANTA UNIVERSITY CONFERENCES

Du Bois provided an overview of the history and mission of Atlanta University as an institution dedicated to the education of African American children and youth in a chapter contributed to the 1905 edited publication *From Servitude to Service: Being the Old South Lectures on the History and Work of Southern Institutions for the Education of the Negro*. At this time, Atlanta University was part of an educational complex that included a normal school (i.e., first eight grades), a high school, and a college. The college's purpose was to help develop African American intellectual talent and leadership and to supply qualified African American teachers. The campus included six buildings and had produced over 5,000 alumni during its first thirty-five years of existence. The college curriculum included coursework in ancient languages, science and math, English and modern foreign languages, as well as history, sociology, philosophy, and pedagogy.

Addressing the sociology program and the sociological laboratory, Du Bois (1905b, 175) wrote, "The department of Sociology and History has sets of modern and ancient maps and a classroom library with reference works, duplicate text-books and statistical treatises." An analysis of Atlanta University college catalogs covering Du Bois' first tenure at Atlanta University reveals that the Department of Sociology and History curriculum included the following courses: Citizenship; Wealth, Work, and Wages; History; Social Reforms; Sociological Laboratory; and General Sociology and Social Conditions of the Negro. The graduate study was summarized under the heading Graduate Study and Research on Social Problems of the South as Part of the Atlanta Conference (MacLean and Williams, 2005).

Du Bois' two-year program in sociology was grounded in an interdisciplinary approach that integrated history, economics, and the study of society. Undergraduate students were introduced to primary sources and received training in the use of statistics, data collection, and data analysis. They assisted with the collection of data that were included in several of the annual Atlanta University Conference reports (Wortham, 2009b). Graduate students played a more direct role in the work of the Atlanta Sociological Laboratory and the Atlanta University Conferences as the sociology graduate program stressed original research (Du Bois, 1900b).

As the head of the Atlanta Sociological Laboratory and as the editor of the Atlanta University Conference annual report during his first tenure at Atlanta

University, Du Bois envisioned a program where each year a particular aspect of "the Negro problems," like the family, crime, or education, would be selected for in-depth scientific study. Survey instruments were prepared and distributed, and data were collected over a six- to eight-month period. An annual meeting was held to discuss the findings of the selected year-long study, and a final report was published. A list of the annual reports either edited or co-edited by Du Bois is in chapter 1 (Table 1.1).

The first study Du Bois edited investigated activities within the African American community that were associated with social betterment (i.e., the work of churches, secret societies, beneficial and insurance societies, coop-erative business activities, and benevolence). Other topics addressed in the first cycle included business, two studies on education (common school and college), skilled workers (e.g., artisans), the Black Church, and crime. A bibliography of published works on the study of "the Negro problems" was provided in the tenth volume. In the second cycle, Du Bois addressed the concept of race and health disparities, economic cooperation activities, and the Black family, and replicated the 1898 report on social betterment. In 1910, he co-edited the replication of the earlier report on college education. Although Du Bois left Atlanta University in 1910, he was affiliated with the next three annual conference reports as a co-editor with Augustus Dill. The Atlanta University Conference annual reports provided a significant body of empirical data on racial inequality in the United States and the various social issues impacting the African American community.

The Atlanta Sociological Laboratory was a center for social inquiry, where aspects of "the Negro problems" could be studied empirically and policy implications were grounded in scientific fact rather than personal opinion and ideology. Du Bois believed that if the causes and characteristics of inequality could be documented and displayed for public consumption, actions would be taken to rectify these conditions. Du Bois' early sociologi-cal work had a lasting impact on his professional development. In *Darkwa-ter: Voices from within the Veil* (1920, 20–21), Du Bois referred to his first Atlanta University experience as his "real life work" and a period of self-discovery. Here he developed strong friendships, studied the human condi-tion, and confronted and documented American racial inequality. After his initial Atlanta University experience, he was no longer the "cold," detached, "scientific investigator."

The 1904 conference on crime from the first research cycle and the 1906 conference on racial and health disparities from the second research cycle are now summarized as a way of illustrating Du Bois' pioneering empirical work on social issues impacting the African American community. Although Du Bois addressed these issues more than a hundred years ago, these two issues are still relevant today.

Crime

In the 1904 Atlanta University Conference Report, *Some Notes on Negro Crime Particularly in Georgia,* Du Bois addressed the interaction between crime and social status. African American crime was linked specifically to the status inequality inherent in the legacy of slavery and additional structural factors like the demand for prison labor and the failure to provide training centers for troubled youth. A weak link was noted also between crime and literacy. Du Bois (1904d, 8) argued that crime "among Southern Negroes is a symptom of wrong social conditions—of a stress of life greater than a large part of the community can bear." Could it be that Du Bois recognized that a mismatch existed between a group's goal of improving their quality of life and the socially accepted means available to the group to achieve that goal? If so, the resemblance between Du Bois' reflections on crime and stratification, and Merton's (1938) structure-strain theory of deviance is strong. Could Du Bois have been one of the first to note and empirically test the association among crime, poverty, and other forms of structured inequality?

Furthermore, Du Bois was concerned about the quality and accuracy of the 1890 census data on crime. Questions about African American male overrepresentation in the crime data and variations in the reporting of different types of crime were acknowledged. Du Bois (1904d) noted that, although African Americans accounted for one-fifth of the crimes committed, they represented only one-eighth on the total population. Furthermore, four out of five African American prisoners lived in the South, and one out of two African American prisoners were aged 20 to 30. Racial and age biases in crime have remained relevant social issues that continue to be discussed by sociologists and criminologists (Seccombe and Kornblum, 2020).

Turning to state-, county-, and community-level data for Georgia, Du Bois (1904d) observed that crime and population heterogeneity varied directly. Racial differences in the perception of African American crime were revealed through ethnographic reports included in the study. It was noted that Whites were more likely than African Americans to perceive that African American crime was increasing. Looking more specifically at state-level statistics over time, Du Bois (1904d) documented declining trends in the volume of African American crime, the number of lynching cases, and the demand for prison labor. On the other hand, increases in African American literacy and property ownership were recognized, and Du Bois argued that African American crime would continue to decline as the reduction in African American status inequality continued. In essence, Du Bois was articulating what is referred to as the "stratification hypothesis" (Stark, 2007).

A discussion of African American children's perception of laws, the police, and the courts was also included in this conference report. The reconstructed table below (Table 2.1) is based on the survey responses of 1,500 African American children in Atlanta public schools aged 9–15. The data indicate that the majority of these young school-age children had a general understanding of the primary purpose and function of the law and the court system. Seven out of ten children indicated that laws existed to provide protection and some sense of peace or order. Likewise, sixty percent of the younger children surveyed were aware that the courts determine guilt or

Table 2.1.   Young African American Atlanta Public School Children's Perception of Crime (N=1,500)[1]

Survey Topic and Primary Responses	Response	
	Number[2]	Percent
1. Laws are made:		
For protection	583	39%
To keep peace and order	315	21%
To govern or rule people	135	9%
2. Courts exist:		
To determine guilt or innocence	398	27%
To see all laws are obeyed	222	15%
To settle matters	222	15%
For bad people	69	5%
3. Policemen are for the purpose of:		
Arresting people	522	35%
Protecting people	346	23%
4. Policemen are usually:		
Kind	618	41%
Unkind	459	31%
Variable (kind or unkind)	204	14%

1.   The children surveyed were aged 9–15. The survey was probably conducted in 1903. The annual conference addressing crime was held on May 24, 1904.

2. The numbers of responses for each category represent the numbers for the primary responses cited in the report and thus do not total 100 percent. The number of non-responses is not known.

Source: Du Bois, Some Notes on Negro Crime Particularly in Georgia (1904d).

innocence, settle issues, enforce the laws, or provide some type of punishment for persons who misbehave (Du Bois, 1904d). The children were fairly clear about the purpose of policemen but expressed more disagreement when it came to their perception of the police. Again, approximately six out of ten of these younger students believed that a policeman's job was to arrest people and to protect people; however, only four in ten of these younger children perceived the police as being kind (Du Bois, 1904d). Overall, it appeared that these younger children were aware of the purpose and intent of laws, courts, and policemen—three measures of social control.

Social problems are often addressed from cultural and/or structural perspectives. Du Bois (1904d) evoked both approaches in the concluding policy recommendations section where the amount of crime, the causes of crime, and possible cures were addressed along with an appeal to the White community. African American crime was associated with the African American community's marginal social status, the persistence of slavery, limited labor market participation, and a flawed judicial system. Furthermore, the churches, the school system, job training centers, and youth centers could impact African American moral standards in a positive manner, and the White community could partner with the African American community to encourage judicial reform, eliminate the prison labor program, and support prisoner rehabilitation efforts. Again, it was clear that Du Bois believed that reform would flow naturally from the presentation of scientific facts. The major problems were overcoming people's ignorance and fear.

Health Disparities

The demographic focus of the Atlanta University Conference annual reports was showcased in *The Health and Physique of the Negro American*, the official publication of the eleventh conference. The first half of this 1906 publication was devoted to the discussion of race as a social construct. Demographic and health-related concerns were addressed in the second half of the report, where Du Bois included discussions of racial differences in fertility and mortality, racial biases in the insurance industry, African Americans' access to hospitals, current medical training opportunities for African Americans, and the supply of African American health care personnel (Du Bois, 1906c).

With this conference study, Du Bois relied heavily on findings from the 1900 census. A summary of the racial differences in fertility, population composition, and mortality patterns is presented in Table 2.2. In 1850, fertility levels were slightly higher for African American women, but by 1900 the fertility levels for African American and White women were essentially the same. The number of children under age 5 per 1,000 women aged 15–41 was 577 and 581 for African American and White women, respectively.

Based on the total population, the median age for Whites was more than three and a half years higher than that for African Americans. Compared to females in each racial group, higher median ages were recorded for African American and White males, and the racial gap in median age by gender was roughly the same, 3.8 years for males and 3.4 years for females. Youth and elder dependency were similar for African Americans and Whites. According to the sex ratio data, the White population in 1900 was characterized by

Table 2.2. United States Population Dynamics by Race: 1900

Population Characteristic	African Americans	Whites
Fertility		
Children under age 5 per 1,000 women aged 15–41	577	581
Population Composition		
Median Age (Years)		
Total population	19.7	23.4
Males	20.0	23.8
Females	19.5	22.9
Age Dependency (Percentage)		
Population under age 15	39.5	9.0
Population age 60 and above	4.9	5.2
Sex Ratio	99	104
Mortality		
Crude Death Rate (per 1,000 population)		
Total population	29.6	17.3
Urban population	27.6	18.6
Primary Causes of Death (per 100,000 population)		
Consumption	485.4	173.5
Pneumonia	355.8	181.8
Nervous system	308.0	213.7
Infant Mortality Rate		
(deaths under age one per 1,000 population)		
Total population	371.5	158.0
Males	403.9	175.9
Females	339.7	139.8

Source: Du Bois, *The Health and Physique of the Negro American* (1906c); figures are based on data Du Bois obtained from the 1900 Census.

an oversupply of males, while females slightly outnumbered males within the African American population. Du Bois (1906c) attributed this reversal in the African American sex ratio to the legacy of slavery.

Following a framework outlined earlier in the chapter on health in *The Philadelphia Negro* (1899a/1996), Du Bois provided an expanded discussion of mortality. The crude death rate data indicated that sizable racial differences in mortality for both the total population (12.3 deaths per 1,000 population) and urban areas (9 deaths per 1,000 population) existed. Racial differences in the primary cause of death and infant mortality were observed as well. African Americans were almost three times as likely to die from consumption, twice as likely to succumb to pneumonia, and faced a 44 percent higher risk of death from diseases of the nervous system. These data indicated that the major causes of death were attributed to infectious diseases and that in 1900, the United States was still in the early stages of the epidemiological transition. A similar racial mortality pattern was noted with respect to infant mortality. For the total population, the African American infant mortality rate was roughly 2.35 times that for Whites.

Du Bois (1906c) attributed these racial differences in mortality to neglect, poor nutrition among children, unsanitary living conditions, and the involvement of African Americans in more dangerous occupations. He argued that consumption was primarily a "social disease" (i.e., crowd disease) rather than a race-specific disease, and maintained that African American mortality could be lowered if sanitary conditions were improved and if African Americans had access to better educational and occupational opportunities.

Attention turned next to a discussion of the problems African Americans had experienced in acquiring insurance. Du Bois (1906c) noted that insurance companies charged African Americans higher premiums because African American mortality rates were higher relative to Whites and African Americans were more likely to allow their policies to lapse. African Americans were perceived as being a higher-risk group. Referencing a report that was based on the findings obtained from thirty-four insurance companies, Du Bois emphasized that African American mortality rates were lower than those for the Irish population and equal to that for Germans. Consequently, seven Northern states had passed laws preventing race-based discrimination within the insurance industry. Also, given the prejudice and discrimination within the insurance industry, there had been growth in the number of Black-owned insurance companies (Du Bois, 1906c).

The health disparities treatise concluded with a discussion of the state of African American health care. A summary portrayal of available Black health services and the number of trained African American medical personnel is showcased in Table 2.3. While African Americans had access to all hospitals in the North, health care in the South was segregated by race. By 1906, there were 42 private Black hospitals, and many of the general hospitals in the South had segregated wards. Almost half the private Black hospitals (19) were located in North Carolina, Georgia, Tennessee, and Alabama (Du Bois, 1906c).

There were 160 Black drugstores in 1906, and by 1905, African Americans could receive medical training at five medical schools: Howard University Medical Department; Meharry Medical College, Walden University; Leonard Medical School, Shaw University; Louisville National Medical College; and Flint Medical College, New Orleans University. These schools provided training for physicians, dentists, pharmacists, and nurses (Du Bois, 1906c).

While detailed descriptions of each medical program were noted in the conference report, a brief description of Shaw University's Leonard Medical School is provided as an example. The medical complex included four separate structures, and the Leonard medical building included lecture rooms, an amphitheater, a laboratory, and dissecting rooms. A medical dormitory

Table 2.3.   Available Black Health Services and Trained African American Medical Personnel: 1900–1906

Health Service/Personnel	Number
Private Black Hospitals (1906)	42
Black Medical Schools (1905)	5
Black Drugstores (1906)	160
African American Physicians (1900)	
Total	1,734
Male	1,574
Female	160
African American Graduates from Black Medical Schools (1905)	
Physicians[1]	1,252
Dentists	116
Pharmacists	243

1. Du Bois indicates that there were 213 African American graduates from White Northern Medical Schools.

Source: Du Bois, The Health and Physique of the Negro American (1906c); figures are based on the statistical reports that Du Bois obtained for the 1906 Atlanta Conference and data from the 1900 Census.

provided housing for 60 students, and the hospital building was equipped with three wards. The dispensary was housed in another structure. For the 1905–1906 academic year, there were 12 faculty serving 178 students. Most of the students (147) were in the four-year medical program, and 31 students were in the three-year pharmacy program (Du Bois, 1906c).

In 1900, the number of African American physicians in the United States totaled 1,734, of whom 91 percent were male; however, by 1906 the number of African American physicians had declined slightly. According to available 1905 data, there were 1,252 African American graduates from the five Black medical schools, and 213 African Americans had graduated from Northern medical schools. Also, the Black medical schools had graduated 116 dentists and 243 pharmacists by 1905 (Du Bois, 1906c).

In this Atlanta University Conference annual report, Du Bois (1906d) provided examples of the prejudice and discrimination experienced by African American medical personnel and medical students. First, he noted that the Southern Dental Association grew out of the National Dental Association since many African American dentists who were in positions of authority acknowledged that they were not respected by Southern White dentists. Likewise, African American students were not allowed admission to many of the medical programs in the Border States and in the South (Du Bois, 1906c). For example, Baltimore Medical College released a statement acknowledging, "We have never had a Negro pupil in the Baltimore Medical College. One such pupil would, I am sure, be a great injury to our class on entering" (Du Bois, 1906c, 90). The Medical Department of the University of Georgia issued a harsher statement: "There are no niggers in this school and there never have been and there never will as long as one stone of its buildings remains upon another" (Du Bois, 1906c, 90).

The health disparities conference publication concluded with a resolutions section. Here Du Bois (1906c) indicated that available statistical data confirmed that African American mortality had declined over the 1890–1900 decade, and that racial differences in mortality varied by the quality of life experienced by the respective racial groups. Also, while African Americans had experienced greater access to health services, more hospitals and medical personnel were needed. Finally, the conference encouraged the African American community to establish local health leagues. These health leagues would promote the advantages of preventive medicine and better sanitation.

Du Bois' efforts to integrate theory and methods enabled him to define and establish the scientific basis of sociology's scope. This approach to sociological investigation was illustrated in the Atlanta University Conference annual reports. Attention shifts now to a review of Du Bois' analysis of quality of life in Philadelphia's Seventh Ward.

NOTE

1. Some of the material included in this chapter is based on material published previously in 2005 as "The early sociological legacy of W. E. B. Du Bois," in A. Blasi (Ed.), *Diverse histories of American sociology* (74–95). Leiden: E. J. Brill. The material incorporated has been revised and permission to include the revised previously published material has been obtained from Brill.

CHAPTER 3

Philadelphia's Seventh Ward

A Demographic, Urban Sociological Investigation

The study of population size, composition, the spatial distribution of population characteristics, and population dynamics is an important cornerstone of demography.[1] For example, in Wirth's (1938) classic study on urban life, he argued that urban populations can be distinguished in terms of their size, density, and social and cultural heterogeneity. A population's gender and age composition matter also. Some researchers maintain that gender power and the sex ratio are inversely correlated (Guttentag and Secord, 1983), while others argue that religious participation rates are stimulated where populations are characterized by an oversupply of females (Finke and Stark, 2005; Stark, 2004). Du Bois (1899a/1996, 1906c) commented on the oversupply of females within the African American community at the turn of the twentieth century.

Addressing variations in key population characteristics like educational attainment and the elder and youth dependency ratios within the Southern Black Belt, Wimberley and Morris (1997) demonstrated why it is important to be able to specify regional patterns in quality of life. Furthermore, population dynamics can transform an area. Over sixty years ago, the area that became Research Triangle Park, North Carolina was a sparsely populated area characterized by rural farmland and hunting grounds at the outskirts of Durham, Raleigh, and Cary. Today, it is an international research center. Finally, quality of life is impacted by the interaction among health, longevity, and social status (Marmot, 2004).

Population studies have been a part of the development of the American sociological tradition from the discipline's beginning. In his historical study of American sociology's early years, *American Sociology: The Story of Sociology in the United States through 1950*, Odum (1951) referenced two Columbia University Ph.D. dissertations as representing the first sociologically based studies on population. The first dissertation was a 1915 study by W. S. Thompson, "Population: A Study in Malthusianism," and the second was a 1920 study on "Negro Migration" by T. J. Woofter, Jr. Odum also devoted several pages of his study to outlining Du Bois' emphasis on "practical sociology," the development of sociology as an academic discipline, his empirical approach to sociological research, and his work on race and ethnicity. However, his contributions to population studies and demography were not acknowledged.

STUDYING URBAN NEIGHBORHOOD TRANSITION

Du Bois' contributions to the development of urban sociology follow a similar pattern of neglect. In *There Goes the Neighborhood* (2006), William Julius Wilson and Richard Taub provide a comprehensive discussion of racial, ethnic, and class conflict in four transitional Chicago neighborhoods and demonstrate how these conflicts impact neighborhood social organization and the quality of life. Residents who have become dissatisfied with the changing quality of life may choose to "exit" the neighborhood once a transitional "tipping point" has been reached, or they may perceive exiting as being too costly, while others may have been able to maintain a sense of loyalty to the neighborhood and choose to remain. This last group has chosen to exercise what Albert Hirschman calls "voice." Persons exercising voice are willing to address the changes being experienced and are willing to build a new sense of unity within the context of growing neighborhood diversity. Thus, businesses, block groups, civic groups, churches, and political groups become "ours" rather than "theirs."

Wilson and Taub's study blended quantitative and qualitative approaches to data collection and analysis and provided an effective demonstration of methodological triangulation as a research design. Census data were utilized to identify broad general trends in population composition, family structure, family income, poverty, educational attainment, labor force participation, and occupation. However, an ethnographic approach was employed to provide a more accurate portrayal of the "pulse" and "character" of each community (Wilson and Taub, 2006). The ethnographers utilized in the two-and-a-half-year study also assumed the roles of participant observers as community, block-club, and religious meetings were attended to capture aspects of the different communities' strength and disorganization.

Commenting on the decision to integrate quantitative and qualitative approaches to data collection and analysis, Wilson and Taub (2006, 191–192) maintain that their study represents "the first time, to our knowledge, that social scientists have systematically used ethnographic methods to conduct a comparative community study—that is, to study several neighborhoods at the same time, collecting comparable data for analysis." Perhaps the claim is valid if the emphasis stays on the simultaneous ethnographic study of several urban neighborhoods. However, a framework for their approach was provided by W. E. B. Du Bois, over one hundred years earlier, in his seminal sociological study of urban life, *The Philadelphia Negro* (1899a/1996), and, even in this study, he commented occasionally on quality of life issues impacting other wards in Philadelphia in addition to the Seventh Ward.

In *The Philadelphia Negro*, Du Bois (1899/1996) presented his early "trademark" approach to sociological research design, methodological triangulation. Census data were utilized to document primary trends in racial inequality throughout Philadelphia, and, where appropriate, comparative census statistics were provided. A more comprehensive view of the quality of African American life in this urban setting was obtained from the five-schedule survey of Philadelphia's Seventh Ward. The five schedules included a family schedule, an individual schedule, a home schedule, a street schedule, and an institutional schedule. There was also a house-servant schedule. The data collected from this last schedule was utilized by Isabel Eaton to provide her report, "Special Report on Negro Domestic Service in the Seventh Ward Philadelphia," which was attached to Du Bois' larger study. Ethnographic data were obtained also so that quantitative and qualitative data could be interfaced to provide more nuanced information related to housing conditions, different social class experiences, poverty, and crime as well as racial prejudice and discrimination within Philadelphia's Seventh Ward. While Du Bois did not conduct extensive analyses of other Philadelphia wards, his comments on African American quality of life, interspersed throughout the study, indicate that he had an awareness of living conditions in other parts of the city.

In *The Philadelphia Negro*, Du Bois addressed such demographic concerns as population size, composition, and growth as well as urban quality of life, racial variations in mortality, access to affordable housing, educational opportunities, and livable wages. The wide range of social issues addressed in *The Philadelphia Negro* confirms why W. E. B. Du Bois was a pioneering figure within the emerging fields of demography and urban sociology at the turn of the nineteenth century and well into the twentieth.

A DEMOGRAPHIC PORTRAIT OF URBAN LIFE IN PHILADELPHIA'S SEVENTH WARD

On June 6, 1896, Du Bois received an offer from Provost C. C. Harrison at the University of Pennsylvania to conduct a comprehensive study of Phila- delphia's African American community residing in the Seventh Ward. Du Bois was granted a one-year appointment as an "assistant" in sociology and received $900 remuneration (Aptheker, 1997). His sole purpose was to con- duct a research study. Consequently, he lived in the Seventh Ward, did not teach any classes, had only one encounter with students, and was not listed in the college catalogue. The only mention of Du Bois' involvement with the university was found in Samuel Lindsay's "Sociological Field Work" course description. Lindsey was a member of the university's sociology faculty (Katz and Sugrue, 1998).

The Philadelphia Negro (1899a/1996) is one of the earliest empirically based sociological studies of urban life in the United States. It is a clas- sic study of urban ecology, urban ethnography, and urban social problems (Anderson, 1996). In terms of methodological sophistication, this study rivals Durkheim's *Suicide* (1897/1966), as Du Bois' study is based on historical contextual data, census data, survey data, and ethnographic data. Myrdal (1944) identified *The Philadelphia Negro* as the definitive study on race relations at the time. Du Bois' "letter of credentials" indicated that he was to conduct a study of the social and living conditions of "Colored people" living in the Seventh Ward, where he would investigate such topics as lifestyle, occupational opportunities, and children's educational involve- ment. The goal was to compile "accurate statistics" that would provide a basis for reform (Aptheker, 1997).

Employing a triangular methodological approach, Du Bois was following a research design that had earlier characterized Booth's (1892–1897) study of everyday life in London, Addams' (1895) Hull-House studies, and the Col- lege Settlement Association's surveys of low-income populations in major U.S. cities (Bobo, 2007; D. Lewis, 2009; Broderick, 1958). The survey of the Seventh Ward was conducted over a fifteen-month period between August 1, 1896, and December 31, 1897. Approximately 9,700 persons and 2, 250 households were included in this door-to-door survey. The five schedules used in the study may have been patterned after the schedules utilized by Booth in his London studies. Also, Du Bois appears to have been aware of Booth's "double method," whereby persons were subdivided by district (i.e., place of residence) and occupation (D. Lewis, 2009).

Interview data were obtained from housewives, landlords, and neighbors and lasted from ten minutes to an hour. He warned his readers against overgeneralizing the findings from the Seventh Ward and indicated that deceptive answers, omissions, and judgment errors represented potential sources of bias. Du Bois attempted to minimize researcher bias by personally conducting all the interviews (Babbie, 2016); however, biases based on his personal judgment remained. The motivation for the study was Du Bois' desire to document "the truth despite its possible unpleasantness" (Du Bois, 1899a/1996, 3). Du Bois believed that the study could provide a scientific basis for future social reform.

Demographic Conditions

The demographic part of the study began with a discussion of African American population growth throughout the nineteenth century. Utilizing available census data, Du Bois (1899a/1996) noted that between 1790 and 1890, African Americans comprised less than five percent of Philadelphia's total population and that the percentage composition had declined over time. Likewise, since 1820, a surplus of women had characterized the African American community. This surplus was attributed to more women having access to industrial jobs and employment in domestic service. However, between 1820 and 1890, the sex ratio increased from 71 to 89 as it appeared that more males were securing jobs also as servants.

An ethnographic and geographic description of the Seventh Ward followed the discussion of population growth. Businesses and residences were located to the north while working class and middle-class residences flanked the southern border. African American, Italian, and Jewish slums were to the east, and industries and residential neighborhoods were located farther west. One of the slum areas was described as follows:

> The alleys near, Ratcliffe street, Middle alley, Brown's court, Barclay street, etc., are haunts of noted criminals, male and female, of gamblers and prostitutes, and at the same time of poverty-stricken people, decent but not energetic.

There is an abundance of political clubs, and nearly all the houses are practi-
cally lodging houses, with a miscellaneous and shifting population. (Du Bois,
1899a/1996, 60)

A more affluent area was described in the following manner:

Passing up Lombard, beyond Eighth, the atmosphere suddenly changes,
because these next two blocks have few alleys and the residences are good-
sized and pleasant. Here some of the best Negro families of the ward live.
Some are wealthy in a small way, nearly all are Philadelphia born, and they
represent an early wave of emigration from the old slum section. (Du Bois,
1899a/1996, 60)

Later, in describing Philadelphia's four worst slum wards (i.e., the Fourth,
Fifth, Seventh, and Eighth Wards), Du Bois indicated that these wards
included a large new immigrant population. However, on several different
occasions, he maintained that the African American slums were experiencing a high rate of population turnover as more affluent African Americans
were moving out (Du Bois, 1899a/1996, 60–61, 78, 81, 151, and 154). Wilson (2012) described a similar situation within Chicago's Black community
in *The Truly Disadvantaged*, whereby African American middle-class and
upper-class residents in the downtown urban neighborhoods migrated to
the suburbs, leaving a disenfranchised African American urban underclass
behind. Du Bois' discussion of class-based migration in and out of the slum
areas anticipated the "theory of ethnic succession" formulated and presented
by Park, Burgess, and McKenzie in their classic 1925 study, *The City*, by
twenty-five years!

A demographic portrait of the Seventh Ward based on Du Bois' analysis
of the survey data he collected is provided in Table 3.1. These data reveal
that the Seventh Ward's African American population was characterized by
a surplus of women (i.e., sex ratio = 87.0), and over half of the population
of males and females was age 30 and under. Slightly more females were
under age 20 while the age 20 and over population included a larger proportion of males. More than half the ward's population was from the South
(54.3 percent), and only a third of the population (32.1 percent) was native
to Philadelphia. Also, slightly more than half (53.3 percent) of the population had resided in the ward for less than ten years. Du Bois described a
migration stream that involved young working-age male adults coming from
the rural areas of the South to small Southern towns and then migrating to

Table 3.1.   Demographic Profile of the African American Population for Philadelphia's Seventh Ward, 1896–1897

Demographic Characteristic	1896–1897 Survey
Total African American Population	9,675
Sex Ratio	87.0
Gender and Age Composition	
Males	
Under Age 20	23.4%
Ages 20 to 30	28.3%
Age 30 and over	48.3%
Females	
Under Age 20	25.4%
Ages 20 to 30	27.9%
Age 30 and over	46.7%
Birthplace	
Philadelphia	32.1%
Pennsylvania, outside Philadelphia	6.0%
South	54.3%
New England and Middle States	5.3%
West or Foreign	2.3%
Migrants' Length of Residence	
Under 5 years	28.8%
5–9 years	24.5%
10–20 years	21.4%
21 years or more	25.4%

Source: Du Bois, The Philadelphia Negro (1899a/1996).

larger Southern cities like Norfolk and Richmond. The migration chain then extended to Washington, DC, Baltimore, and finally Philadelphia. Upon arrival in Philadelphia, these rural South migrants settled in slums, where economic opportunities were limited. In essence, Du Bois was describing a prelude to the "Great Migration" of African Americans from the rural South to the urban North from 1910 to 1970.

Social and Economic Conditions

Addressing social support networks, Du Bois (1899a/1996) argued that the Black Church strengthened the African American community by enhancing educational opportunities, providing benevolent aid when needed, providing a venue for social and cultural activities, as well as providing encouragement and strengthening moral standards. Within the Seventh Ward, seven out of ten families specified a particular religious identity.

Racial differences in mortality were addressed in the chapter on health, where Du Bois maintained that the racial difference in mortality in Philadelphia could be attributed primarily to differences in living conditions and social class. The African American crude death rate for the Seventh Ward for the 1884–1890 period was 30.5 deaths per 1,000 population, while the White rate was 24.3 deaths per 1,000 population (Du Bois, 1899a/1996). Du Bois observed that the leading causes of death for African Americans were consumption (TB), diseases of the nervous system, pneumonia, and heart disease. For Whites, the first two causes changed places. At this time Philadelphia had not experienced the epidemiological transition as more persons were dying from infectious diseases. As noted in chapter 2, Du Bois argued that consumption was primarily a "social disease" (i.e., crowd disease) that could be attributed to such factors as poor ventilation, dampness, limited outdoor activities, climate, limited access to medical services, and heredity. Moving in a social policy direction, he concluded the chapter on health by calling for the African American community to advocate for improved housing and sanitation conditions, better quality food, and greater access to fresh air (Du Bois, 1899a/1996).

Additional family structure and socioeconomic characteristics for Philadelphia's Seventh Ward are displayed in Table 3.2. First, one notes that males in the Seventh Ward were more likely to be married or single. On the other hand, women were significantly more likely to be either widowed or permanently separated from their husbands. Du Bois (1899a/1996) noted that limited economic resources particularly impacted the quality of family life of young married couples and those widowed. Gender differences in life expectancy would have increased the proportion of females widowed as well.

The average family size for residents of the Seventh Ward was five persons, and one-third of families resided in one-room dwellings. Families often included unrelated lodgers, along with young married couples without children, and grandparents keeping their grandchildren. Economic pressures kept family size low. The illiteracy rate for African Americans residing in the Seventh Ward was 12.2 percent, and only a small proportion of men or women were engaged in manufacturing and mechanical industries. The dominant occupational status was domestics and personal service. The survey data revealed that 61.5 percent of males and 88.5 percent of females were engaged in domestic and personal service (Du Bois, 1899a/1996).

Table 3.2. Social and Economic Characteristics of Philadelphia's Seventh Ward: 1896–1897

Social/Economic Characteristic	Seventh Ward
Family Structure	
Marital Status (persons aged 15 or more)	
Males	
Single	41.4%
Married	52.5%
Widowed/Permanently Separated	6.1%
Females	
Single	30.5%
Married	47.1%
Widowed/Permanently Separated	22.4%
Average Family Size	5.1
Living Space[1]	
Families living in one room	35.2%
Families living in two–five rooms	32.8%
Families living in six or more rooms	32.0%
Socioeconomic Status	
Education	
Total population illiterate	12.2%
Occupational Status	
Males	
Agriculture	0.3%
Professional Service	2.5%
Domestics and Personal Service	61.5%
Trade and Transportation	28.0%
Manufacturing and Mechanical Industries	7.7%
Females	
Agriculture	0.0%
Professional Service	1.4%
Domestic and Personal Service	88.5%
Trade and Transportation	1.3%
Manufacturing and Mechanical Industries	8.8%
Family Income[2]	
Very Poor–Poor (weekly earnings $5 or less)	18.5%
Fair–Working Class (weekly earnings $5–$9.99)	47.8%
Comfortable–Good/Middle Class (weekly earnings $10–$19.99)	29.5%
Well-to-Do (weekly earnings $20 or more)	4.2%
Housing Monthly Rent Payment[3]	
Under $5	21.9%
$5–$9.99	28.7%
$10– $19.99	28.3%
$20 or more	21.1%
Lodging System[4]	
Own/rent home–live alone	31.0%
Own/rent home–lodgers/sub-rent	38.0%
Sub-rent under other families	31.0%

1. Percentages are based on data for 2,355 families.
2. Percentages are based on data for 2,276 families.
3. Percentages are based on data for 2,235 families.
4. Percentages are based on data for 2,441 families.

Source: Du Bois, *The Philadelphia Negro* (1899a/1996).

Du Bois stratified the families residing in the Seventh Ward into four classes based on weekly wages (Table 3.2). As noted in chapter 2, the weekly income for the "very poor and poor" families was $5 or less. Approximately one in five families (18.5 percent) were included in this lowest-income category. Almost half of the Seventh Ward's families (47.8 percent) were classified as "fair" or working-class families who earned $5 to $9.99 weekly, and almost three in ten families (29.5 percent) were identified as middle class (i.e., "comfortable–good"), where family members collectively were earning $10 to $19.99 weekly. The most affluent families, the "well-to-do," represented less than five percent (4.2 percent) of all families. Here, total weekly family income was $20 or more.

Monthly housing costs could represent a large expense based on the weekly wages cited above. This could impact a family's ability to find suitable housing or own or rent a residence without having to open the home to lodgers or sub-rent the residence to other families. One in five families (21.9 percent) paid under $5 a month for housing, and half the families (50.6 percent) paid under $10 a month. Slightly less than one-third of the families (31.0 percent) were able to own or rent their home and did not sub-rent to lodgers or sub-rent under other families (Table 3.2).

The Seventh Ward did experience some economic growth. This was seen primarily in the entrepreneurship efforts that Du Bois was able to document. Within the Seventh Ward, community members offered a range of basic economic services, and Du Bois (1899a/1996) was able to identify 118 businesses. The top five Black businesses were: restaurants (N=39), barber shops (N=24), shoemakers (N=13), grocery stores (N= 11), and cigar stores (N=11). Collectively, these five enterprises accounted for 83.1 percent of all Black businesses in the Seventh Ward. While these businesses catered primarily to the African American residents in that ward, business exchanges were not necessarily limited to African American patrons, and Black business enterprises were beginning to serve persons beyond the Seventh Ward.

In the concluding chapters of *The Philadelphia Negro*, Du Bois sought to shed further light on the reality of prejudice and discrimination in the City of Brotherly Love (*philos adelphos*). He navigated these realities by requesting that Philadelphia's African American community and White community work together to begin resolving "the Negro problems." Du Bois cited numerous examples where members of Philadelphia's African American community faced difficulty obtaining employment and keeping their jobs.

African Americans encountered an occupational caste system and were generally relegated to lower-status positions. Discrimination was encountered in public places like restaurants, stores, recreational facilities, and public schools. The degree of meaningful social interaction ultimately was regulated by the parameters set by "the color line" (Du Bois, 1899a/1996).

Calling upon Philadelphia's African American and White communities to cooperate in addressing these issues, Du Bois encouraged the African American community to: 1) insist that educational opportunities be provided for their children; 2) save money, and 3) purchase homes. As African American families and Black Churches worked together, the community's moral fiber could be strengthened and social activities for young people could be provided. On the other hand, the White community would need to address the persistence of race-based prejudice and discrimination. Du Bois concluded the study by reminding Philadelphians that social uplift (i.e., social mobility) and the eradication of prejudice and discrimination were not mutually exclusive events.

By the end of 1897, Du Bois completed his work for the University of Pennsylvania and accepted a position at Atlanta University, where he directed the work of the Atlanta Sociological Laboratory, coordinated and provided oversight for the annual Atlanta Conferences for the Study of the Negro Problems, and contributed to the building of a program of undergraduate and graduate instruction, which provided a foundation for enhancing sociological investigation. His insistence on the scientific study of "the Negro problems" was taking root at the same time that sociological programs were being developed at Columbia and Chicago (Wright, 2002a; 2002b; Odum, 1951).

Given his commitment to empirical sociology and to the training of a new generation of scholars and researchers, it is not surprising that Du Bois wanted to know how data involving African Americans would be collected going forward. His concerns were formally expressed in a 1900 article, "The Twelfth Census and the Negro Problems," published in *The Southern Workman*. Du Bois (1900c) believed that the U.S. Census was the proper government agency to collect and disseminate reliable data on African American quality of life. He maintained that census studies could be combined with small area studies to address topics like population composition and distribution, occupational structure, marital status, mortality, education, crime, and land ownership. As noted in chapters 1 and 2, Du Bois addressed many of these topics in the various Atlanta University Conference annual reports during his first tenure as a sociologist at Atlanta University.

Du Bois (1900c) concluded the article by recommending that persons working with the twelfth census collaborate with a "Special Committee for the Study of the Negro Problems." He argued that the measure for race needed further specification as persons of African descent should not be aggregated with the Japanese and Indians. Furthermore, a separate volume of statistics on the African American population based on 1900 census data should be generated, and a series of studies exploring such topics as occupation and wages, property ownership, education, and crime could be completed. These studies would provide baseline empirical data that could be utilized in subsequent research.

NOTE

1. Some of the material included in this chapter is based on material that was published previously as "W. E. B. Du Bois' Urban Sociology." *Sociation Today* 6.3 (2008). www.ncsociology.org/sociationtoday, and "W. E. B. Du Bois and Demography: Early Explorations." *Sociation Today* 7.1 (2009). www.ncsociology .org/sociationtoday. The material incorporated in this chapter has been revised, and permission to include the revised, previously published material has been obtained from the editor of *Sociation Today*.

CHAPTER 4

Rural Sociology

The Farmville, Virginia Social Study

Taking a summer break from his massive urban-based study of African American quality of life in Philadelphia and Philadelphia's Seventh Ward, Du Bois spent July and August of 1897 in Farmville, Virginia—a small rural community. Here, he administered a twenty-one-item questionnaire to Farmville's African American residents. This survey was a shortened version of the more extensive Philadelphia survey, which had been based on five schedules. However, many of the same quality of life issues were addressed as Du Bois sought to collect empirical data on such topics as population composition, marital status, family size, home ownership, educational attainment, occupational structure, annual income, and religious identification. These data were enriched with available census data and ethnographic descriptions based on Du Bois' personal observations. This small area sociological study was published in 1898 in the *Bulletin of the Department of Labor* and is the rural sociology counterpart to his book-length urban sociological study, *The Philadelphia Negro* (1899a/1996).

W. E. B. DU BOIS AND CARROLL WRIGHT

Carroll Wright, a well-known statistician, served as the first Commissioner of the U.S. Department of Labor from 1885 to 1905. Wright was interested in investigating the working conditions of African American laborers. He believed this could be accomplished by collecting a reliable body of labor statistics (Grossman, 1974). For Wright, statistics provided the foundation upon which "practical sociology" could be based. In his sociology text, *Outline of Practical Sociology* (1900), Wright distinguished sociology and practical sociology. For Wright, sociology's primary goal was to provide an explanation for how human institutions have originated and developed, whereas practical sociology's task was to assess current social conditions by accumulating a body of statistical facts. Thus, in the chapter on criminology, Wright addressed such issues as statistical methodology and the study of crime, local conditions and crime, economic conditions and crime, as well as labor and crime. In analyzing social issues, Wright noted that it was important to identify relevant social (i.e., family, church, and labor) and political (i.e., state, city, town, and county) units.

Du Bois took a similar approach to the study of society and social problems. In "The Study of the Negro Problems," Du Bois (1898a) framed the scientific study of "the Negro problems" within a social problems framework. Here a social problem was portrayed as a mismatch existing between a group's actual environmental setting and its desired status. Du Bois argued that a careful study of "the Negro problems" would be grounded in the documentation of the historical development of a particular social issue and an empirical study of current social conditions related to the issue integrating statistical analysis, anthropological description, and sociological analysis. This approach would provide an empirical basis for social reform. Here the impact of Gustav Schmoller and the Historical School of Economics upon Du Bois' thought is evident (Zamir, 1995; Boston, 1991). Du Bois' preference for the inductive method and what Wright termed "practical sociology" is stated clearly in the opening remarks of the Farmville study. Du Bois (1898b, 1) proclaimed, "In this work there has been but the one object of ascertaining, with as near an approach to scientific accuracy as possible, the real condition of the Negro." Consequently, when Wright contacted Du Bois in February 1897 about studying African American industrial development, Du Bois responded affirmatively. A meeting was held in Washington in March, and Du Bois provided more detailed proposals in additional correspondence during May and June. The foundation for what was to become the Farmville study was outlined in a letter to Wright dated May 5, 1897 (Aptheker, 1997).

Du Bois proposed two paths of action and offered some additional suggestions for further research on African American industrial development (Aptheker, 1997). Plan A called for a study of economic conditions of one to five thousand African Americans in Virginia, the Carolinas, or Georgia by addressing such issues as wages, occupations, home ownership, and cost of living. The study would be like the study of Philadelphia's Seventh Ward and would be conducted during July and August of 1897. Data would be obtained from a survey, county records, and personal observations. African American involvement in various trades was the focus of the second proposal (Plan B). This study could be carried out in Richmond, Raleigh, Charleston, or Atlanta. Plans for other projects included more extensive studies of African American involvement in the professions, the Negro Church, farm laborers, organized labor, and the economic condition of African Americans since Emancipation. Several of these projects were eventually addressed by Du Bois in latter publications for the Department of Labor's *Bulletin* (Du Bois, 1899b; 1901a), the annual Atlanta University Conferences on the Study of the Negro Problems (Du Bois, 1899c, 1902b, 1903d/2003, 1907b, and 1912 with Dill) and other journal and book publications (Du Bois, 1911a 1911b, 1911c/2007, 1935/2007).

Du Bois indicated that Plan A could be carried out "immediately" and could be the first in a series of studies on the economic conditions of African Americans in small areas (Aptheker, 1997). Farmville, Virginia was selected as a representative community, and Wright agreed to provide financial support for the project if he was satisfied with the final product (Grossman, 1974). Du Bois produced an acceptable product, and he went on to publish studies on African Americans and the Black Belt (Du Bois, 1899b), African American landholders in Georgia (Du Bois, 1901a), and African American farmers (Du Bois, 1904a) while Wright was still the Commissioner of Labor.

Between 1897 and 1903, the U.S. Department of Labor published nine studies on African American labor (Grossman, 1974). A tenth study for the series was conducted by Du Bois in 1906 and involved an extensive study of the social, economic, and political conditions of African Americans residing in Lowndes County, Alabama. This study is the topic of chapter 5, where a partial reconstruction of the study is provided. The massive survey-based study was completed but was never published. Du Bois (1968/2007) considered this study to be one of his best examples of sociological work and believed that it was suppressed for political reasons. At this point, Du Bois' ties with the Department of Labor came to an end, and the Department of Labor also discontinued its study of African American labor (Grossman, 1974).

THE FARMVILLE STUDY AND METHODOLOGICAL TRIANGULATION

The Farmville study, a classic study in rural sociology and small area, community studies, begins with a general discussion of Prince Edward County followed by a brief overview of the town of Farmville. Located near the state's geographic center, Prince Edward County was part of Virginia's Black Belt and was known for its high level of tobacco production. Farmville was the county seat and led the state in the production of tobacco strips (Du Bois, 1898b). The community was portrayed as being "gossipy and conservative" and functioned as a "clearing house" (Du Bois, 1898b, 4–5). Industrial opportunities attracted young workers from the adjacent rural counties, but many of Farmville's youth had migrated and would be migrating to larger Southern and Northern cities in search of jobs.

Census data were identified to document changes in the county's and town's population and to specify farm size, acreage under cultivation, and the amount of primary agricultural products produced at the county level. U.S. Census data on age structure, marital status, occupational classification, and family size were cited throughout the report to provide a comparative context for interpreting the Farmville survey data. While much of the data for Farmville was derived from the twenty-one-item questionnaire, real estate assessments were obtained from the county clerk's office, and a cost-of-living profile was constructed from patterns noted in the purchasing records obtained from three Farmville grocers serving the local African American community. Qualitative data were secured from Du Bois' personal observations and conversations with schoolteachers and townspeople (Du Bois, 1898b). Employing a triangular methodological research design, Du Bois was able to utilize empirical data from a variety of different sources to provide a more comprehensive portrait of the social and economic living conditions of Farmville's African American community.

In the Farmville study, and in several of his early writings, Du Bois (1897b, 1898b, 1899a/ 1996, 1900d, 1903d/2003) noted that the Black Church served more than a religious purpose. In addition to preserving important aspects of African tribal culture, the church functioned as the educational, economic, and social center of the community. The church was also an agent of social uplift and reform, and offered moral guidance for the community. Consequently, he could be very critical of the church's leadership. In the Farmville study, Du Bois provided the following assessment of two local ministers.

> Both are graduates of theological seminaries and represent the younger and more progressive element. They use good English and no scandal attaches to their private life, so far as the investigator could learn. Their influence on the

whole, good, although they are not particularly spiritual guides, being rather social leaders or agents. Such men are slowly but surely crowding out the ignorant but picturesque and, in many particulars, impressive preacher of slavery days. (Du Bois, 1898b, 16−17)

Du Bois' remarks reflected his dislike for the older, more emotional preaching styles.

While the church was the key institution within the African American community, Du Bois did not view the African American community as a homogeneous social and economic group and was one of the earliest sociologists to acknowledge this (Morris, 2007). Furthermore, Du Bois (1897b) believed that healthy social activities and work strengthened character. At the end of the Farmville study, Du Bois provided a general description of three distinct classes within Farmville's African American community. Only the social life of the highest class was described. Du Bois (1898b, 36) described a country picnic enjoyed by this class: "At another time there was a country picnic on a farm 20 miles from town. The company started early and arrived at 10 o'clock on a fine old Virginia plantation, with manor house, trees and lawn. The time was passed in playing croquet, tossing the bean bag, dancing, and lunching."

The game of croquet functions as a cultural and social marker, and provides further evidence of the existence of class stratification within the African American community. Other social stratifiers include educational attainment, occupation, family income, home ownership, and household size. Du Bois relied on the collected survey data to denote trends among these variables. The survey was administered to 1,225 individuals and 262 families and addressed such topics as age, sex, marital status, family size, length of residency, literacy, length of school term, occupation, wage income, unemployment, property and home ownership, and church attendance. While Du Bois was able to obtain answers from respondents for most of the questions, errors in the data were unavoidable, and some questions were associated with a higher margin of error than others. Information derived from the questions on age and number of persons in the family was less reliable as were the data on annual family income. In the latter instance, earnings were estimated based on available data on wages from certain occupations, seasonal employment opportunities, and normal expenditures for basic commodities like food, fuel, clothing, and lifestyle choices (Du Bois, 1898b).

Once again, Du Bois' use of a triangular methodology is systematically unveiled in this small area social study of a rural Virginia community. Survey data were utilized to identify general trends in African American quality of life while census data were introduced to provide a context for the comparative analysis of group similarities and differences. Ethnographic descriptions were provided to specify nuances in the quantitative data. Again, Du Bois institutionalized this blending of quantitative and qualitative approaches to research within the nascent field of scientific sociology.

DEMOGRAPHIC AND SOCIAL CHARACTERISTICS OF AFRICAN AMERICANS RESIDING IN FARMVILLE

Du Bois utilized the data obtained from the twenty-one-item survey to provide a profile of the African American community residing in Farmville at the end of the nineteenth century. The data acquired are discussed under three general headings: demographic characteristics, socioeconomic status, and family and group life. A portrait of the quality of life of African Americans residing in Israel Hill is provided as a separate analysis. Located on the outskirts of Farmville, this small African American farming community occupied land that was originally owned by John Randolph and was given by Randolph and other family members to former slaves when they were emancipated (Du Bois, 1898b).

Demographic Characteristics

Demographers are generally concerned with such issues as population size, population composition (i.e., sex ratio and age–sex–pyramid), the spatial distribution of a population and quality of life characteristics, and population dynamics (i.e., mortality, fertility, and migration). While Warren Thompson's 1915 dissertation on Malthus and Thomas Woofter's 1920 dissertation on African American migration are generally regarded as the first two book-length demographic studies by sociologists (Odum, 1951), Du Bois' Farmville essay represents an earlier primer on demographic description. As noted in chapter 3, Du Bois offered an even more extensive treatment to similar demographic issues in *The Philadelphia Negro* (1899a/1996), as entire chapters were devoted to such topics as "The Size, Age and Sex of the Negro Population" (chapter 5), "Conjugal Condition" (chapter 6), "Sources of the Negro Population" (chapter 7), and "The Health of Negroes" (chapter 10).

The topics addressed in Du Bois' demographic overview of Farmville, VA included population change, racial composition of the population, age and sex composition, place of birth, marital status, illegitimacy, crude birth rates and crude death rates, infant mortality, and miscegenation. Selected demographic statistics addressing population size, composition, and marital status are summarized in Table 4.1.

Farmville's African American population had grown steadily from 1850 to 1890; however, Du Bois' survey findings indicated that Farmville's African American population had experienced a slight decline from 1890 to 1897. With the beginning industrialization of the South and the economic infeasibility of small farm agriculture under the crop lien system, persons had been migrating from the farming districts of rural counties like Prince Edward County to small communities like Farmville in search of skilled labor opportunities in local industries such as tobacco stripping. Likewise, persons reared in Farmville but unable to find year-round work would migrate to larger cities like Richmond, Baltimore, and New York. Again, Du Bois was documenting an early wave of the later "Great Migration" (1910–1970) of African Americans from the rural South to the urban North.

Turning to population composition, one notes that African Americans comprised three-fifths of Farmville's total population. This presence was relatively stable as the African American share of Farmville's total population had ranged from 56 percent to 61 percent since 1850 (Du Bois, 1898b).

Table 4.1. Demographic Characteristics of Farmville's African American Community, 1897

Category/Indicator	Measure
Population	
Total African American population, 1897	1,225
Total African American population, 1890	1,443
African American population as percent of total population, 1890	60.0
Population Composition	
Sex Ratio	95.4
Marital Status	
Males	
Percent African American males aged 20 and over married, Farmville	65.4
Percent African American males aged 20 and over married, U.S. (1890)	69.0
Percent native White males aged 20 and over married, U.S. (1890)	66.1
Females	
Percent African American females aged 20 and over married, Farmville	55.0
Percent African American females aged 20 and over married, U.S. (1890)	65.0
Percent native White females aged 20 and over married, U.S. (1890)	67.9

Source: Du Bois, "The Negroes of Farmville, Virginia: A Social Study" (1898b).

Du Bois is one of the earliest sociologists to document and address the low sex ratio within the African American community. In Farmville there were roughly 95 African American males to every 100 African American females. This was well below the 1900 sex ratio of 104.4 for the total U.S. population (United States Census, 2007) and 98.6 for all African Americans (Stark, 2007). Du Bois attributed this low sex ratio to the migration of males to Northern cities in search of employment.

The 1897 Farmville data and the national data on marital status for 1890 for males by race were comparable. With respect to cross-national data obtained from Mayo-Smith's *Statistics and Sociology* (1895), the marriage rate for Farmville's African American males was comparable to the rate for males in Germany and Italy and higher than that for males in Ireland. However, Du Bois discovered that, relative to females, Farmville's African American males aged 20 and over were more likely to be married (65.4 percent versus 55.0 percent). This finding is not surprising given the surplus of females in Farmville created by the out-migration of males. Du Bois noted further that unfavorable economic conditions were contributing to a delay in marriage, and low marriage rates could be attributed to a combination of structural (e.g., employment and migration) and cultural (e.g, moral standards) factors. The focus on structural and cultural factors distinguished Du Bois' approach to social issues and inequality from latter sociological approaches, which have been more prone to emphasize either structural factors (Wilson, 1996, 2009) or cultural factors (O. Lewis, 1966; Patterson, 2000). Like Durkheim (1897/1966), it appears that Du Bois understood that strong communities were a function of a high degree of social and moral integration.

Socioeconomic Status

Socioeconomic status is one of the most utilized indicators of inequality. It is generally operationalized as an index based on three variables: education, occupation, and income. Du Bois addressed each of these indicators of socioeconomic status in the Farmville study. Early in his sociological career, Du Bois (1898b, 1899a/1996) maintained that racial inequality and prejudice were grounded in ignorance. Consequently, he strove to provide a sound body of empirical evidence, which would document racial inequality and provide an empirically based framework to stimulate social change. Data on educational attainment, occupational classification, and annual family income derived from the Farmville survey are presented in Table 4.2.

Table 4.2. Socioeconomic Status of Farmville's African American Community, 1897

Category/ Indicator	Measure	
	Number	Percent
School Attendance (Aged 5–15)		
Males	192	56.3
Females	175	55.4
Illiteracy by Age		
Persons aged 10–20 years	319	22.6
Persons aged 21–40 years	298	29.2
Persons aged 41 or more	272	72.1
Occupational Classification (Aged 10 and above)		
Professional	22	2.4
Commercial	45	4.9
Industrial	282	30.5
Agricultural	15	1.6
Domestic Service	287	31.1
Unemployed	259	28.0
Not reported	14	1.5
Annual Family Income by Social Class (N=Families)		
Poverty	29	11.1
Moderate	128	8.9
Comfortable	63	24.0
Well-to-Do	42	16.0

Source: Du Bois, "The Negroes of Farmville, Virginia: A Social Study" (1898b).

Farmville's African American children attended a district school. Young males and females aged 5–15 were equally likely to attend school, but only a little more than half the children attended school. Of those who attended school, only half attended the normal six-month school term since many of the children worked in the tobacco stripping factories (Du Bois, 1898b). The lower levels of educational attainment that were associated with the Black Belt region in the 1997 study by Wimberley and Morris were also present in Du Bois' Farmville study one hundred years earlier. However, Du Bois (1898b) documented one significant educational gain with respect to the age-group data for literacy. Three distinct generations are identified in these data: 1) the slavery generation, which included persons aged 41 or more; 2) persons aged 21–40, who grew up during the Civil War and Reconstruction; and 3) persons aged 10–20, who were part of the current generation. Illiteracy declined dramatically as one moved from the generation born into slavery (72.9 percent) to those who were born during the Civil War–Reconstruction period (29.2 percent).

Employment opportunities are identified as a key structural factor impacting African American quality of life. Migration, delayed marriage, property ownership, and race relations were all linked by Du Bois to employment opportunities. In addition to experiencing limited employment opportunities, African American workers were often paid less than Whites. Du Bois (1898b) argued that prejudice and discrimination were an outcome of status inequality. Apparently, he was aware that Farmville's African American community reflected a low-wage workforce. Once again, Du Bois' analysis seems to foreshadow Wilson's (2009; Wilson and Taub, 2006) work on the association among status inequality, prejudice, and discrimination, and Bonacich's (1972, 1976) studies on the association among the split labor market, economic conflict, and prejudice.

Three distinct categories dominated the occupational classification data for persons aged 10 and above (Table 4.2). Each category accounted for roughly 30 percent of the labor force. The largest group consisted of persons employed in domestic service (31.1 percent). These jobs were primarily held by women and were perceived as a relic of the past and as an employment stereotype. The transition from farming to industrial work was reflected in these data as well. Only 15 individuals made a living from agriculture, while three in ten persons were employed in industry. Most industrial workers were employed in one of Farmville's sixteen tobacco-stripping establishments (Du Bois, 1898b). Rather than growing tobacco or working on a tobacco farm, a significant portion of Farmville's African American workers were employed in the processing of tobacco. Families did, however, maintain their own vegetable gardens.

Twenty-eight percent of Farmville's African American population aged 10 and above were unemployed. These data are disturbing given the fact that most of the tobacco-stripping establishments operated only six months out of the year. Anticipating the arguments of Merton (1938) and the structure-strain theory of crime, Du Bois (1898b) linked crime with poverty and unemployment and noted that Farmville's criminal element was beginning to migrate North in search of work. He concluded that African American crime could be studied best in the context of small communities and that crime rates could be minimized if African American workers had access to steady employment and fair wages (Du Bois, 1898b).

On a more positive note, Du Bois provided several examples where Farmville's African American workers were experiencing less racial tension on the job, a degree of pay equity, and entrepreneurial success. He noted that there were instances where African American and White mechanics worked in the same jobs without experiencing racial tension even though wages were not equal. However, at the "foundry" African American and White workers received similar wages (Du Bois, 1898b). African Americans were also entering new fields like the grocery business and the operation of bakeries and hotels. Farmville's most successful African American entrepreneur was a brick maker. His accomplishments are summarized below in what is apparently an example of exchange mobility.

> The entire brick making business of Farmville and vicinity is in the hands of a colored man—a freedman, who bought his own and his family's freedom, purchased his master's estate, and eventually hired his master to work for him. He owns a thousand acres or more of land in Cumberland County and considerable Farmville property. In his brickyard he hires about 15 hands, mostly boys from 16 to 20 years of age, and runs five or six months a year, making from 200,000 to 300,000 brick. His men receive about $12 a month, and extra pay for extra work. (Du Bois, 1898a, 17)

While "the Negro problems" were grounded in racial inequality, Du Bois (1898b) was quite aware that class differences existed within rural and urban African American communities. In the Farmville study, Du Bois (1898b) placed families in one of the following four classes: well-to-do (16.0 percent), comfortable (24.0 percent), moderate (48.9 percent), and poverty (11.1 percent). The moderate class was the largest class, as 128 (48.9 percent) of Farmville's 262 families were identified as being in this class. Families were placed in one of these four social class categories based on Du Bois' personal observations and on estimates of three sample budgets provided by three local grocers. These estimates were derived from what was considered to be typical expenditures for three essential items: food, fuel, and clothing.

Family and Group Life

While family income impacted the quality of African American life in Farmville, Du Bois expanded his discussions of the African American family by addressing such issues as average family size by family type, size of family dwellings, and dwelling (i.e., home) ownership. He believed that communities were strengthened and solidified through group activities like church involvement and membership in secret and benevolence organizations. Data

Table 4.3.   Family and Group Life among Farmville's African American Community, 1897

| Category/ | Measure | | |
Indicator	Mean	Number	Percent
Average Family Size (Persons) by Family Type			
Possible Family	10.79		
Real Family	5.03		
Economic Family	4.61		
Rooms in Family Dwelling (N=Families)			
1 Room		17	6.5
2 Rooms		134	51.1
3 Rooms		45	17.2
4 Rooms or more		66	25.2
Dwelling Owners by Dwelling Size (N=Families)			
1 Room		3	17.6
2 Rooms		25	18.7
3 Rooms		31	68.9
4 Rooms or more		55	83.3
Black Church Religious Economy (N=Families)			
Baptists		218	83.2
Methodists		26	9.9
Presbyterians		3	1.1
Episcopalians		1	0.4
Not Reported		14	5.3
Secret and Benevolence Organizations (N=Persons)			
Benevolent Society		40–50	
Odd Fellows			35
Randolph Lodge of Masons			25
Good Samaritans		25	
True Reformers		50	

Source: Du Bois, "The Negroes of Farmville, Virginia: A Social Study" (1898b).

on these additional aspects of family life and organizational involvement are shown in Table 4.3.

The definition of the family has sparked sociological debate. Should the family be characterized by common residence, economic activity, and reproduction as Murdock (1949) argued, or is the family essentially a kinship unit charged with the task of socializing its younger members (Reiss, 1988)? Should the definition of family structure be expanded to include extended, nuclear, female and male single parent, and grandparent and grandchildren families as well as cohabiting and same-sex unions?

In a similar vein, Du Bois begins the discussion of family life in Farmville by expressing concern over how family size can be determined best. Data were collected on family size based on three different measures of family size. First, the economic family is a general measure that includes related and unrelated persons living in one dwelling as a family. Second, the possible family is based on the number of parents and the number of children ever born who are still living. Third, the real family includes parents and the number of children currently living in the dwelling (Du Bois, 1898b). Depending on the measure employed, the average size for Farmville's African American family (Table 4.3) varied from 10.79 persons for the possible family to 4.61 persons for the economic family. Given the significant migration of young adults and parents to Northern cities in search of employment, Du Bois maintained that the economic family understated family size. Since the data for the possible family were incomplete, Du Bois (1898b) argued that more weight should be given to the real family (i.e., 5.03 persons) and economic family (i.e., 4.61 persons) measures.

Slightly more than half (51.1 percent) of Farmville's African American families lived in two-room dwellings while one out of four families lived in a dwelling with four or more rooms (Table 4.3). Du Bois (1898b) noted that most of the two-room dwellings were small tenements. The living room was often downstairs, and the kitchen was upstairs. The average room size was 15 to 18 square feet and included two windows. Although half of Farmville's African American families lived in these two-room tenements, only 18.7 percent owned these two-room dwellings. However, dwelling ownership and dwelling size are positively correlated. Smaller dwellings involving one or two rooms were rented while larger dwellings that included three or more rooms were more likely to be owned. Five out of six African American families (83.3 percent) living in dwellings with four or more rooms owned their dwelling. Irrespective of dwelling size, 43.5 percent of Farmville's African American families owned the dwelling in which they were living (Du Bois, 1898b). Thus, home ownership probably functioned as a social class marker. Du Bois (1908a) provided a more detailed description of family life and living conditions in rural and urban communities in the 1908 Atlanta University Conference study on the African American family.

Turning to a discussion of group life, Du Bois began by providing a functional analysis of the role of the Black Church in the African American community. He is the first sociologist to provide a sociological analysis of the Black Church (Du Bois, 1897b, 1898b, 1899a/1996), and the first sociologist to provide an empirically based sociological analysis of a religious group (Wortham, 2005a; 2018b; Zuckerman, 2002). Addressing the religious life of Farmville's African American community, Du Bois maintained that the

Black Church was the center of the African American experience integrating religious, social, intellectual, economic, and moral life. In addition to providing moral guidance, the church sponsored educational opportunities, provided benevolent aid, and sponsored social events (i.e., amusements). Du Bois was thus in agreement with Durkheim (1897/1966, 1912/1995), another contemporary sociologist who argued that religion was a source of social cohesion, a social glue.

The community was revitalized periodically through annual revivals, which were usually held in August. While Du Bois (1898b) disliked these more emotional expressions of religion, he maintained that the community was becoming more resistant to these more traditional, emotional services. However, because of these annual revival meetings, many young people were converted at an early age. Here Du Bois is among the earliest sociologists to observe what is known as "the age factor" in religious conversion (Johnstone, 2016).

A family's religious preference by denomination is presented in Table 4.3. In essence Du Bois depicted the Farmville Black Church religious economy. A religious economy is the set of religious groups operating within a given geographic area, and the religious economy (i.e., religious marketplace) may be regulated or deregulated (Stark and Finke, 2002). The study of religious economies and their impact on religious pluralism and religious involvement has been a topic of debate among sociologists of religion adopting supply-side and demand-side approaches to the study of the religious marketplace (Jelen, 2002).

Baptists and Methodists had been strong in the South since the 1850s (Finke and Stark, 2005). Du Bois' religious identification survey data underscored this trend. Approximately five out of six (83.2 percent) African American families in Farmville identified as Baptist while one in ten families (9.9 percent) was Methodist. It appears that identification with a religious group was expected, as only 14 of Farmville's 262 African American families failed to provide a specific religious group identification. Perhaps Du Bois was among the first to document what later sociologists of religion have described as the semi-involuntary nature of religious participation among African Americans (Ellison and Sherkat, 1995; Nelsen and Kanagy, 1993).

There were three Black Churches in Farmville in 1897, two Baptist and one Methodist. Du Bois provided an ethnographic description of the First Baptist Church of Farmville.

It owns a large brick edifice on Main street. The auditorium, which seats about 500 people, is tastefully finished in light wood with carpet, small organ, and stained-glass windows. Beneath this is a large assembly room with benches. This building is really the central clubhouse of the community. . . . Various organizations meet here, entertainments and lectures take place here, the church collects and distributes considerable sums of money, and the whole social life of the town centers here. (Du Bois, 1898b, 34–35)

Additional commentary on the social functions of the Black Church was shared by addressing such issues as seating capacity, church furnishings, the relationship between the congregation and the community, social activities, alliances with other organizations, and the church budget. He also commented on the more relaxed worship experience and the social networking that often took place at many church-sponsored gatherings (Du Bois, 1898b). Again, Du Bois was ahead of his time, as many of these issues are now addressed in church and community evaluations that are sponsored by various denominational groups and are known as "congregational studies" (Woolever and Bruce, 2010; Ammerman, Carroll, Dudley, and McKinney, 1998).

In *Bowling Alone* (2020), Putnam comments on the deterioration of social capital in the United States. Declines in political, civic, and religious participation are discussed and attributed to such factors as limited time and financial resources, mobility, technology, mass media, and social media. One hundred years earlier, in the Farmville study, Du Bois (1898b) documented the significant involvement of members of Farmville's African American community in benevolent aid societies. Five different societies were active, with membership ranging from 25 to 50 members (Table 4.3). These organizations existed primarily to provide members of the community with financial assistance in times of distress, such as defraying the costs associated with sickness and funeral expenses.

ISRAEL HILL

As noted earlier, Israel Hill was a small farming district located approximately two miles from Farmville. Twenty-five African American families resided in this rural hamlet in 1897. The total population of the community was 123 persons. All members of this community were African American. A social and demographic portrait of the community is presented in Table 4.4.

Table 4.4. A Socio-Demographic Profile of Israel Hill's African American Community, 1897

Category/ Indicator	Measure	Number	Percent
		Response	
Population Characteristics			
Total population		123	
Sex ratio			108.5
Native to Israel Hill		57	58.0
Marital Status by Gender			
Males aged 20 and over married		14	36.8
Males aged 20 and over married (not reporting removed)			53.8
Females aged 20 and over married		16	41.0
Females aged 20 and over married (not reporting removed)			61.5
Illiteracy by Age			
Aged 10–20 years		6	26.1
Aged 21–40 years		5	33.3
Aged 41 or more		21	58.3
School Attendance by Gender			
Males aged 5–15 attending		8	47.1
Females aged 5–15 attending		6	54.5
Occupational Classification by Gender			
Males Age 11 and over			
Laborers/Tobacco factory		9	18.4
Trades/Artisans		4	8.2
Waiter		1	2.0
Farm related		17	34.7
At home or at school		6	12.2
Not reported		12	24.5
Females Age 11 and over			
Tobacco factory		3	6.5
Day worker/Domestic servant		3	6.5
Farmer		4	8.7
Housewife and working		2	4.3
Housewife		13	28.3
At home or at school		8	17.4
Not reported		13	28.3
Family Characteristics			
Home Ownership (N=Families)		22	88.0
Rooms in Family Dwelling (N=Families)			
1 room		7	28.0
2 rooms		9	36.0
3 rooms		3	12.0
4 rooms		6	24.0
Average Family Size (economic family/persons)	4.9		

Source: Du Bois, "The Negroes of Farmville, Virginia: A Social Study" (1898b).

Although Du Bois warned the reader against overgeneralizing the findings obtained from this small number of cases, one can identify trends in the data. Approximately six of every ten current Israel Hill residents had lived there all their life. Compared to Farmville (Table 4.1), Israel Hill's (Table 4.4) sex ratio was much higher (108.5 versus 95.4). The high sex ratio was attributed to a larger male population aged 29 and under. Among this age group, males outnumbered females 37 to 22 (Du Bois, 1898b). However, Israel Hill's population aged 20–29 included eleven males and two females, and only twelve persons (i.e., three males and nine females) were aged 30–49. Du Bois (1898b) suggested that many of Israel Hill's young adults had moved to Farmville or other towns and cities in search of work in industry or domestic service.

It was becoming increasingly more difficult for Israel Hill's residents to earn a living from smallholder agriculture. This is observed in the occupational data for males aged 11 and above (Table 4.4). Seventeen males (34.7 percent) indicated that they were engaged in farm-related activities, but nine male residents were engaged as laborers or tobacco factory workers (18.4 percent) and another 12 persons (24.5 percent) failed to identify an occupation. The largest proportion of females either indicated that they were housewives (28.3 percent) or did not identify an occupation (28.3 percent). Female involvement in domestic service, day work, farming activities, or the tobacco factory was limited, and 17.4 percent of females were at home or at school (Du Bois, 1898b).

Compared to males aged 20 and over, Israel Hill's females of the same age were slightly more likely to be married, and females aged 5–15 were more likely to be attending school (Table 4.4). The school attendance rates for African American females in Israel Hill (54.5 percent) and in Farmville (55.4 percent) were comparable; however, the discrepancy among males in Israel Hill (47.1 percent) and Farmville (56.3 percent) was wider (Tables 4.2 and 4.4). The lower attendance rate among Israel Hill's males was probably due to their involvement in farming activities at an early age. However, illiteracy was less pronounced among Israel Hill's younger age groups. This confirms the trend noted among Farmville's African American residents by age group (Table 4.2).

As might be expected, given the history of the community's origins, home ownership in Israel Hill was high. While nine out of ten families (88 percent) owned their own home, living quarters were small (Table 4.4).

Approximately two-thirds (64 percent) of Israel Hill's families lived in one- to two-room dwellings. Small dwelling size would be associated also with smallholder agriculture (Du Bois, 1899b, 1908a). Only one in four families (24.0 percent) lived in a dwelling with four or more rooms (Du Bois, 1899b). For Du Bois, Israel Hill was an example of a small Southern community in economic transition. Some of the residents were trying to make a living as farmers, but smallholder farming was becoming a less viable option. Persons unable to make a living in agriculture migrated to small towns and more urbanized areas in search of employment in industry or domestic service.

SIGNIFICANCE OF FARMVILLE STUDY

Minority groups may experience neighborhood segregation as an outcome of prejudice and discrimination and consequently may be concentrated in specific geographic locations. However, within these neighborhoods residents may begin to establish a firm economic base by developing services that meet the needs of the residents in this concentrated area. As these entrepreneurial services become more profitable, economic activities expand to meet the needs of the larger community. Portes (1987) referred to this process as the development of "economic enclaves."

Writing ninety years earlier, Du Bois suggested that similar social dynamics were operating in Farmville at the end of the nineteenth century. African Americans were residing in highly segregated neighborhoods. They sponsored their own churches and social activities, and Whites were encountered primarily in the workplace. Farmville's African American community was beginning to develop business ventures that would serve their own needs, and they were becoming more selective in determining the businesses they would patronize. This development minimized the economic dependence of Farmville's African American community on Whites. Consequently, a race-based system of economic dependence was beginning to interface with a system of economic interdependence. Du Bois (1898b, 1899a/1996) believed this shift would improve race relations.

The Farmville study was the rural counterpart to *The Philadelphia Negro* (1899a/1996), a massive urban study of African American quality of life published a year later. Like the Philadelphia study, the Farmville study was based on the utilization of a triangular methodology. Historical, survey, census, and ethnographic data were incorporated to address important social and demographic issues. Several of Du Bois' contributions to the development of American sociology were unveiled in the Farmville study. These pioneering contributions were made in the areas of the sociology of race, social problems, small area studies, rural sociology, the Black Belt, and the sociology of religion.

The Farmville study is the work of an optimistic young sociologist. At this point in his career, Du Bois believed that racial prejudice and inequality were grounded in ignorance. If a body of empirical information could be amassed, a solid foundation for social reform would be made clear. We now turn our attention to the partial reconstruction of the unpublished Lowndes County, Alabama social study. This was Du Bois' last major survey-based study designed to document racial inequality in the Black Belt. Following this unsatisfactory effort, Du Bois' primary focus would shift away from empirical sociology and toward public sociology.

CHAPTER 5

A Black Belt Study

The Unpublished Lowndes County Survey

The Lowndes County, Alabama social study was based on a house-to-house canvass of social and economic conditions to be obtained from approximately 6,000 African American families. The study was authorized by the U.S. Bureau of Labor, and a two-page schedule was printed. This study was to be the fourth study involving African American quality of life in the Black Belt by Du Bois that was sponsored by the Bureau of Labor. The other three were the 1898 Farmville, Virginia study (Du Bois, 1898b), the 1899 study of six different locations within the Black Belt (Du Bois, 1899b), and the 1901 county-level study of Georgia (Du Bois, 1901a). The Lowndes County study was authorized in 1906; data were collected; a report was written, but the study was never published. Du Bois devoted two pages to the discussion of this study in each of his two book-length autobiographies, *Dusk of Dawn: An Essay Towards an Autobiography of a Race Concept* (1940/2007) and *The Autobiography of W. E. B. Du Bois: A Soliloquy on Viewing My Life from the Last Decade of Its First Century* (1968/2007). The second autobiography was published posthumously.

Employing a triangular methodology once again, the study was based on a historical overview of social and economic development in Lowndes County, an investigation of official records, and a house-to-house survey. Du Bois was assisted in the data collection by Monroe Work and R. R. Wright, Jr., two first-generation African American male sociologists. Local workers from Lowndes County were employed also. The Calhoun Colored School served as the headquarters for the investigation and several members of the school staff assisted. According to the summary accounts provided by Du Bois in the two autobiographies, the survey schedules were disseminated, and the results were tabulated. Chronological land maps were created; the crop lien system was studied, and specific data on population distribution, occupational status, political organization (i.e., registered voters), and family life were obtained. According to Du Bois, the study was not published because it addressed sensitive political issues like voter registration and its associated literacy requirements. Du Bois asked for the return of his manuscript but was told that it had been destroyed (Du Bois, 1940/2007, 1968/2007).

Although the study was never published, it is possible to utilize U.S. Census data to discuss some of the topics that were addressed in the study. Thus, the historical pattern of population changes for Lowndes County from 1830 to 1910 can be documented. Demographic data for Lowndes County's African American community addressing males of voting age, literacy, school attendance, and number of farms are available from the 1910 Census. Also, data on religious affiliation and membership in Lowndes County are available via the *1906 Census of Religious Bodies*. Furthermore, Du Bois shared information on Lowndes County in three articles that were published in 1906, 1912, and 1913. A copy of the Lowndes County Schedule prepared by the Bureau of Labor exists, and 60 correspondences detailing various aspects of the Lowndes County study from 1902 to 1909 are accessible. The correspondences are part of the W. E. B. Du Bois Papers, which are included in the Special Collections and University Archives of the University of Massachusetts Amherst Libraries.

To provide a partial re-creation of this study, data on Lowndes County from other articles published by Du Bois are presented first. This is followed by the creation of and discussion of relevant census data based on the three sources noted above. These data are presented in Table 5.1, Table 5.2, and Table 5.3. The 1906 survey schedule that was published by the Bureau of Labor is summarized next. This schedule verifies the types of data that were collected. In the last section of this chapter, the sixty correspondences related to the Lowndes County study are presented in a summary table (Table 5.4). The table includes the date of the correspondence, the communication parties, and the topic or topics addressed in that particular communication. More detailed information contained in some of the communications is then presented by year or group of years to provide additional chronological details of some of the issues related to the scope, cost, and authorization of the study as well as the concerns associated with the coding of the data, data quality issues, and the final outcome of the project.

DATA FROM OTHER PUBLISHED STUDIES

In a 1906 article in *Publications of the American Economic Association*, Du Bois discussed the involvement of the Calhoun Colored School in a local cooperative land-buying venture that began in 1897. Covering the 1897–1906 period, Du Bois reported that approximately 100 African American men were trying to purchase land in Lowndes County and that 72 warranty deeds controlling 3,000 acres of land were currently held in the county. The following data were provided on the number of African American houses based on the number of rooms: 23 one-room houses, 34 two-room houses, and 29 three- or more room houses. There was also a school that met for eight months a year. Du Bois (1906d) noted that 75 African American families were paying taxes on property valued at $25,000; however, none of the African American men associated with these properties could vote under the current Alabama laws.

Additional data on the Lowndes County cooperative land-buying project were provided in a 1912 article in *American Statistical Association Publications*. Here Du Bois addressed voter disfranchisement while providing data on property ownership. His 1906 visit to Lowndes County was mentioned, and he noted that since 1895, African Americans in Lowndes County had purchased 400 acres of land that was valued at $26,793. It was acknowledged also that an additional 630 acres were being acquired and that African Americans had spent $41,536 on the purchase of new homes (Du Bois, 1912).

Once again, Du Bois returned to the theme of African American men's voter registration in Lowndes County in his 1913 article titled "Social Effects of Emancipation." In 1900, Du Bois had stated that 1,057 White males aged 21 and over were literate while the number of African American males in the same category was 1,788! However, from 1902 to 1906 the number of registered African American voters increased from 39 to 52 while the number of White registered voters increased from 1,097 to 1,142. The Alabama educational requirement for voting is referenced once again as being a major cause of voter suppression (Du Bois, 1913).

Through these three articles, Du Bois was able to provide data on the African American community's quality of life in Lowndes County. More specifically, data were provided on land ownership, value of property, house size, value of new homes, schools, literacy, voter registration, and voter disfranchisement. These are topics that Du Bois was trying to address in more detail in the Lowndes County social study.

CENSUS DATA AND THE SURVEY SCHEDULE

Following the pattern initiated in the Farmville, Virginia social study, Du Bois would have presented historical census data on population growth in Lowndes County, Alabama. Decennial census data are available beginning in 1830, and Du Bois would have showcased data from 1830 through 1900 and estimated the data for 1906. Given that the bulk of the survey data collection and the investigation of public records would have taken place from 1906 and into 1908, total population data are presented in Table 5.1 for the county from 1830 to 1910. Data for the African American population are provided for 1890, 1900, and 1910.

The total population of Lowndes County increased steadily from 9,410 persons in 1830 to 35,651 persons in 1900. Throughout this period, African Americans represented the largest population group. In 1890, African Americans comprised 85.5 percent of the county's total population, and by 1910 African Americans represented 88.2 percent of the county's total population. From 1900 to 1910 many African Americans left the rural South and moved to the urban North. This out-migration stream was a prelude to the "Great Migration" from 1910–1970. Du Bois documented this development in the Farmville study and in *The Philadelphia Negro*. This out-migration apparently was beginning to take place in Lowndes County as the African

Table 5.1. Population of Lowndes County, Alabama: 1830–1910

Year	Total Population	African American	Percent Population African American
1830	9,410	—	—
1840	19,539	—	—
1850	21,915	—	—
1860	27,719	—	—
1870	25,719	—	—
1880	31,176	—	—
1890	31,550	26,985	85.5
1900	35,651	30,889[1]	86.6
1906[2]	33,395	29,233	87.5
1910	31,894	28,125	88.2

1. This information was supplied by Du Bois in a communication with Charles Neill, U.S. Commissioner of Labor, dated 1/19/1906.

2. Estimates for the total population and the African American population for 1906 are based on a 10-year linear decline.

Source: Population of States and Counties of the United States: 1790–1990 in Lowndes County, Alabama Population 2022. https://worldpopulationreview.com. Accessed June 6, 2022. United States Census Bureau. *1910 Census*. Volume 2. Population Reports by States, with Statistics for Counties, Cities, and Other Civil Divisions: Alabama–Montana. Census. gov/library/publications/1913/dec/vol-2-population.html.

American population declined from 30,889 persons in 1900 to 28,125 persons in 1910. The African American population decline (2,764 persons) represented 73.6 percent of the total population decline (3,757 persons); however, the concentration of the African American population in the county increased during this ten-year period as the percentage of the total population who were African American rose from 86.6 percent to 88.2 percent.

Given a total population of Lowndes County in 1900 of 35,651 persons and of 31,894 persons in 1910 and given that the rate of population decline from 1900 to 1906 is linear, the projected total population in 1906, the time when Du Bois was collecting his survey data, would have been 33,395 persons. Assuming a similar linear rate of population decline for the African American population, the projected African American population would have been 29,233 persons. Based on this estimate, African Americans would have comprised 87.5 percent of the total population. The population decline in Lowndes County has continued as the total population has fallen from 35,651 persons in 1900 to 10,311 persons in 2020. Also, the African American population has declined from 30,889 persons in 1900 to 7,149 persons in 2020 (Table 5.1). African Americans now comprise 69.3 percent of the total population and still represent the largest population group (Lowndes County, Alabama, n.d.; United States Census Bureau, 1913; United States Census Bureau, 2020).

Table 5.2 showcases five demographic indicators for Lowndes County's African American community in 1910. Again, it is noted that African Americans comprised 88.2 percent of the total population in 1910. The second and third indicators address the voting-age population and literacy. Du Bois (1906d, 1912, 1913) had noted in other related essays that African American disfranchisement was an issue of concern. The Lowndes County 1910 census data reveal that there were 6,053 African American males of voting age at the time, and they represented 86.0 percent of all males of voting age. However, 3,541 of the voting age males were illiterate. This represented 58.5 percent of the African American male voting-age population. On the other hand, 2,502 African American males of voting age were literate! This is why Du Bois was questioning the Alabama literacy requirements as they related to voting. Again, Du Bois (1913) had observed that in 1906 only 52 African American males were eligible to vote. Women of any race could not vote at this time.

The 1910 Lowndes County census data also show that 51.1 percent of all African Americans aged 10 and over were illiterate. This is partly due to access to public education and the varying length of the school year. The

Table 5.2.   Demographic Characteristics of the African American Population of Lowndes County, Alabama: 1910

Indicator	Metric
Total African American Population	28,125
Percent of Total Population	88.2
Total Males of Voting Age	7,037
African American Males of Voting Age	6,053
Percent of Males of Voting Age	86.0
Illiterate African American Males of Voting Age	3,541
Percentage of African American Males of Voting Age Illiterate	58.5
African Americans Aged 10 and Over	20,135
Number Illiterate	10,280
Percentage Illiterate	51.1
African Americans Aged 6 to 14	6,786
African American Children Attending School	3,142
Percentage Attending School	46.3
Number of Farms	6,486
Number of Farms African American and Other Nonwhite	5,755
Percentage of Farms African American and Other Nonwhite	89.4

Source: U.S. Census Bureau. *1910 Census.* Volume 2. Population Reports by States, with Statistics for Counties, Cities, and Other Civil Divisions: Alabama–Montana. Census.gov/library/publications/1913/dec/vol-2-Population.html.

percentage of African American children aged 6 to 14 years attending public school was only 46.3 percent. At this time, the major sources for basic education for many African American children in Lowndes County were the home and the Black Church. The 1910 census data indicate also that 89.4 percent of the farms in Lowndes County were owned by African Americans or by other nonwhites (Table 5.2). Given the way the data were reported, it is not possible to determine how many of the farms were African American owned. However, given the significant involvement of the African American community in farming, it is understandable why Du Bois was interested in 1) how the crop lien system operated in the county; 2) how much land was owned or controlled by African Americans; and 3) the value of the land, the crops harvested, livestock, and farm-related equipment.

As noted earlier Du Bois (1897b, 1899a/1996, 1903d/2003) argued that the Black Church was the center of the African American experience. The church functioned as a social support mechanism, an educational system, a benevolent society, and an avenue for preserving and portraying cultural identity. In the Lowndes County study, Du Bois did inquire about church membership. Although the data from the survey were not reported, it is possible to get a glimpse of African American church membership in Lowndes

County in 1906. The source for these data is the *1906 Census of Religious Bodies* published by the United States Census. The government collected data on a decennial basis from 1850 to 1890. After the 1890 publication, data were reported for 1906, 1916, 1926, and 1936. After this point the census no longer collected data on religious bodies. Religious membership data for Lowndes County in 1906 are summarized in Table 5.3.

An area's religious economy is comprised of the different religious groups located within a particular geographic location (Stark and Finke, 2002). For Lowndes County in 1906, membership data were available for eleven different religious groups. Based on an estimated total population for Lowndes County of 33,395 (Table 5.1) and given a total membership in all reported religious groups of 16,338, it is estimated that 45.9 percent of the total population were members of a religious group irrespective of age.

The largest religious group was Southern and National Baptists. These two Baptist groups comprised 67.4 percent (11,010 members) of the total religious group membership. The Southern Baptists are primarily a religious organization serving the White community; whereas, National Baptists would primarily serve the African American community. Four of the mainline Black Church denominations primarily serving the African American community at this time and included in the *1906 Census of Religious Bodies* data in Table 5.3 are the National Baptist, African Methodist Episcopal

Table 5.3. Lowndes County, Alabama Religious Economy: 1906

Christian Group	Total Membership	Percent of Membership
Southern and National Baptists[1]	11,010	67.4
African Methodist Episcopal	128	0.8
African Methodist Episcopal Zion	2,307	14.1
Colored Methodist Episcopal	785	4.8
Primitive Baptists	305	1.9
Disciples of Christ	633	3.9
Church of Christ	400	2.4
Methodist Episcopal South	585	3.6
Presbyterian Church in the U.S.	84	0.5
Protestant Episcopal	92	0.6
Roman Catholic	9	0.1
All Christian Religious Groups	16,338	100.1

1. National Baptists, the African Methodist Episcopal Church (AME), the African Methodist Episcopal Zion Church (AMEZ), and the Colored Methodist Episcopal Church (CME) are mainline African American denominations.

Source: United States. Department of Commerce and Labor. E. Dana Durand, Director. *Religious Bodies: 1906*. Part 1. Summary and General Tables. Washington, DC: U.S. Government Printing Office, 1910.

(AME), African Methodist Episcopal Zion (AMEZ), and Colored Methodist Episcopal (CME) churches. African American membership in these three Methodist groups would have been 3,220 persons. Collectively these three Black Church denominations accounted for 19.7 percent of the county's total religious group membership. When the Methodist Episcopal South Church, a White denomination, is added to the mix, one discovers that Methodists represented the second-largest religious group in Lowndes County, accounting for 23.3 percent of all religious group membership. Collectively these two major denominational groups accounted for 90.7 percent of all religious group membership. The dominance of Baptists and Methodists in Lowndes County in 1906 was a pattern noted throughout the South and the nation at the time as well (Finke and Stark, 2005).

The data on Lowndes County presented in Tables 5.1 through 5.3 are public data. Du Bois could have had access to some of these data along with historical records and included them in his report on the social and economic conditions experienced by African Americans residing in Lowndes County, Alabama in 1906. However, what specific data was Du Bois trying to collect? Fortunately, a copy of the Lowndes County survey schedule is included in the W. E. B. Du Bois Papers that are part of the Special Collections and University Archives of the University of Massachusetts Amherst Libraries. It appears that the schedule was printed in 1906 (Du Bois, 1906e) and that data were collected from fall 1906 through January 1907 (Table 5.4, communication dated 2/5/1907).

The Lowndes County survey was designed to collect data that would provide a comprehensive, empirically based assessment of the state of African American farming in a specific Deep South location. Data were collected on the following topics:

- numbers of persons in the household (space for up to ten persons)
- sex, age, and birthdate of individuals
- marital status
- literacy
- race
- persons not currently present
- educational attainment
- housing characteristics (e.g., number of rooms)
- land (acreage and amount owned or rented)
- equipment liens

- type of crops harvested (amount and value)
- monetary advances received (amount and debt)
- organization membership (e.g., church)
- deaths since last Christmas
- general remarks

After the majority of the data were collected in 1906, the next two years (1907–1908) were spent analyzing the data and addressing questions about data inconsistencies and the overall quality of the data. The title of the final report produced was "Negro Labor in Lowndes County, Alabama," and Du Bois was paid $1,000 for his efforts (Du Bois, 1908b, 1908c). A November 9, 1908 memorandum indicated that the report would be published in the Bureau of Labor's *Bulletin* in January 1909 (Du Bois, 1908d). However, in what appears to be the last correspondence related to the publication of the Lowndes County study (April 22, 1909), Du Bois responded to an inquiry by Henry Farnam, stating:

> The manuscript which has been in Dr. Neill's hands for over a year now is much too long for publication and must be edited. My plan was to have it put in shape as would suit the Labor Bureau and then send a revised copy to you. Meantime, however, there has been much delay in getting the matter by the Labor Bureau and it is a question as to whether or not they will publish it. (Du Bois, 1909a)

Unfortunately, this study, Du Bois' last major attempt to provide an academic, empirical study on "the Negro problems," was never published.

CORRESPONDENCES: 1902 TO 1909

Attention now turns to the 60 correspondences related to this study. These correspondences bear witness to the fact that the study was authorized, carried out, questioned, and never published. The number of communications by year is as follows:

- 1902 (1)
- 1903 (3)
- 1904 (1)
- 1905 (5)

- 1906 (10)
- 1907 (24)
- 1908 (15)
- 1909 (1)

Ten of the correspondences occurred between 1902 and 1905. All five of the 1905 documents are drafts of study proposals. Another ten correspondences are associated with 1906, the year the study was authorized, the survey schedule was produced, and the majority of the data was collected. Du Bois visited Lowndes County in 1906. Thirty-nine of the sixty correspondences (65.0 percent) occurred between 1907 and 1908, the period where the accuracy of the data collected was questioned and the report was submitted. The only correspondence for 1909 is the one just noted, where Du Bois questioned whether the study would ever be published. Seventeen of the correspondences were between Du Bois and Charles Neill. Neill became the commissioner of labor in 1906 and was serving in this capacity at the time of the last study correspondence in 1909. Another eight correspondences were between Du Bois and John Lemon, who was a staff member at the Calhoun Colored School. This school served as the headquarters for the study. Seven of the communication exchanges were between Du Bois and G. W. W. Hanger, who served as acting commissioner of labor during parts of 1906 and 1907. In Table 5.4 the individual correspondences are presented chronologically; the communicators are identified, and the major topic or topics addressed are summarized.

While Table 5.4 contains a summary of the specific communication topic or topics discussed in the sixty correspondences, each of the communications is not discussed in detail here. Rather, a discussion of some of the specific details about the study's scope and the problems associated with the quality of the data collected that are contained in selected correspondences is given within the context of the following chronological groupings: 1902–1904, 1905, 1906, 1907, and 1908–1909.

1902–1904

The interest in a social study on African American quality of life in Lowndes County, Alabama began with an inquiry by Du Bois to Carroll Wright, the Commissioner of the United States Bureau of Labor, on July 25, 1902. Wright indicated that he may be able to authorize a study for the 1903 fiscal year (Du

Table 5.4. Lowndes County, Alabama Social Study Communications: 1902–1909

Date	Parties	Communication Topic
1902 (N=1)		
7/28/1902	Carroll Wright[1] to Du Bois	Possible study authorization for 1903.
1903 (N=3)		
1/2/1903	Du Bois to Walter Wilcox[2]	Black Belt farming, wages, and local conditions.
2/21/1903	Du Bois to Wilcox	Request for data collection schedules for Lowndes County.
No date	Du Bois to Wilcox	Data on eight indicators requested.
1904 (N=1)		
4/18/1904	Du Bois to Wright	Delay of commitment to Lowndes County study.
1905 (N=5)		
No date	Du Bois	Draft of Black Belt county study–five data categories.
No date	Du Bois	Typed version of proposed Lowndes County study with five data categories identified.
No date	Du Bois	Draft of study of farming and industrial conditions in Lowndes County, Alabama, and proposed budget.
No date	Du Bois	Draft of additional indicators for study based on three data collection schedules.
No date	Du Bois	Eight-point memoranda on Lowndes County study.
1906 (N=10)		
1/19/1906	Du Bois to Charles Neill[3]	Request for a house-to-house survey for Lowndes County at a cost of $1,000.
1/22/1906	Neill to Du Bois	Planned meeting with Du Bois to discuss study.
1/23/1906	John Lemon[4] to Du Bois	Estimate of cost for persons to canvass the area.
2/22/1906	Du Bois to Neill	Outline of proposed study.
3/5/1906	Neill to Du Bois	Acknowledgment of receipt of proposal.
6/22/1906	Lemon to Du Bois	Revised cost to canvass area ($1,500 to $2,000).
7/9/1906	Du Bois to Neill	Cost to conduct Lowndes County study revised again ($750 to $1,250).
7/24/1906	G. Hanger[5] to Du Bois	Labor Department caps study costs (including all expenses) at $2,000. Du Bois responds favorably.
No date	Du Bois	Notes on thirteen data categories for proposed study are provided.
No Date	Department of Labor	Two-page Lowndes County Schedule–eighteen data categories.

1. Carroll Wright was the commissioner of labor at this time.
2. Walter Wilcox was a chief statistician at the United States Census Office.
3. Charles Neill became the new commissioner of labor in 1906.
4. John Lemon was a staff member of the Calhoun Colored School in Lowndes County.
5. G. W. W. Hanger was the acting commissioner of labor at the time of this correspondence.

(continued)

Table 5.4. *(continued)*

Date	Parties	Communication Topic
1907 (N=24)		
2/5/1907	Du Bois to Neill	Data collection for schedules completed and franking labels are requested.
2/5/1907	Neill to Du Bois	Twelve address labels are provided.
2/14/1907	Du Bois to Neill	Schedules sent to Neill with data corrections noted on the schedules.
2/16/1907	Du Bois to Bureau of Labor	Memorandum identifying enumerators, coding categories, and comments on answers. Du Bois requests tabulations for twenty-two indicators.
2/18/1907	Neill to Du Bois	Meeting in Washington to discuss tabulations. Copies of corrected schedules are requested, and ten address labels are sent.
2/28/1907	Neill to Du Bois	Du Bois is notified that schedules must be inspected and edited. Only clearly understandable tables will be tabulated. Ten areas of concern are noted, and Du Bois is asked to meet with Bureau statisticians.
3/6/1907	Du Bois to Neill	Du Bois responds to seven of Neill's concerns and will edit the schedules if they are returned.
3/19/1907	Neill to Du Bois	Several of Du Bois' explanations for data discrepancies are accepted. Questions about family, school, and equipment data remain. Again, Du Bois is asked to meet with Bureau statisticians in Washington.
3/22/1907	Du Bois to Neill	Study now exceeds the $1,250 budget allocation. An inquiry about travel funds is made.
3/27/1907	Neill to Du Bois	Cost for the study cannot exceed $2,000. Du Bois must absorb travel costs.
3/28/1907	Pitt Dillingham[1] to Du Bois	Rating of Lowndes County merchants requested. Data on land ownership will be delayed.
4/3/1907	Neill to Du Bois	A meeting with Neill to discuss data schedules on 4/16/1907 is set.
4/29/1907	Henry Farnam[2] to Du Bois	Farnam is willing to review the data before it is submitted to the Bureau of Labor.
4/30/1907	Charlotte Thorn[3] to Du Bois	Information on crop lien system in Lowndes County is requested by Hampton Institute. An inquiry is made concerning the status of the final report on the Lowndes County study.
5/4/1907	Thorn to Du Bois	Du Bois provides responses to questions raised by Hampton Institute.

1. Pitt Dillingham was a staff member of the Calhoun Colored School in Lowndes County.
2. Henry Farnam was a Yale professor and a trustee of the Calhoun Colored School. He was affiliated with the Carnegie Institution of Washington.
3. Charlotte Thorn was a staff member of the Calhoun Colored School in Lowndes County.

Table 5.4. *(continued)*

Date	Parties	Communication Topic
5/8/1907	Du Bois to Hanger	A question concerning the release of the preliminary data tabulations is raised.
5/10/1907	Hanger to Du Bois	Preliminary data tabulations will be delayed to July or August.
5/10/1907	Hanger to Du Bois	Du Bois will receive $1,000 for the materials needed to produce survey report.
5/23/1907	Farnam to Du Bois	Manuscript for review should be sent to the European address provided.
8/30/1907	Hanger to Du Bois	Tabulations are being discontinued because too many irreconcilable data errors exist. Use of available data is uncertain.
9/6/1907	Hanger to Du Bois	Reference is made to Bureau letter of 8/30/1907.
10/8/1907	Du Bois to Neill	Du Bois requests that the schedules be returned to him so that tabulations can be conducted at Atlanta University. Persons who collected the data will be contacted to clarify data errors.
10/8/1907	Mary Ovington[1] to Du Bois	Reference is made to recent conflict between Du Bois and Monroe Trotter. Copy of the Lowndes County study is requested once published.
11/2/1907	Neill to Du Bois	Income data for survey are not reliable for tabular presentation. Data schedules are returned to Du Bois.
1908 (1908=15)		
2/6/1908	Du Bois to Neill	Du Bois will provide an article-length manuscript on the Lowndes County study by 4/1/1908.
4/1/1908	Lemon to Du Bois	Data on four mortgages in Lowndes County are provided.
5/1/1908	Du Bois to Lemon	A copy of Sam Hamilton's mortgage payments for 1897–1905 is presented. There is a reference to a mortgage for Augustus Johnson.
5/4/1908	Lemon to Du Bois	Sam Hamilton is debt-free and awaiting receipt of property deed. Augustus Johnson defaulted on land payments.
5/15/1908	Lemon to Du Bois	There is a reference to a list of Lowndes County churches, but the list is not attached. Lemon states that some churches listed may no longer exist. (Table 5.3 contains data on Lowndes County from the *1906 Census of Religious Bodies*.)
5/25/1908	Lemon to Du Bois	Lemon indicates that his work on the study is finished. Land records will be checked by Edward Whiting.

1. Mary Ovington was a social activist and a writer and was involved in the founding of the NAACP (National Association for the Advancement of Colored People).

Table 5.4. *(continued)*

Date	Parties	Communication Topic
6/3/1908	M. L. Polean[1] to Du Bois	Du Bois is paid $1,000 for the report, "Negro Labor in Lowndes County, Alabama," which was submitted to the Bureau of Labor in May 1908.
6/10/1908	James McCall[2] to Du Bois	The proposed work of "The Alabama Plantation Improvement Society" is discussed. The group was considering focusing its efforts on living conditions in Lowndes County.
6/12/1908	G. W. Esterly[3] to Du Bois	The payment of $1,000 for the Lowndes County study is confirmed.
8/14/1908	Ovington to Du Bois	Ovington questions the status of the Lowndes County study, and Du Bois questions whether the Bureau will publish the study.
10/1/1908	Monroe Work[4] to Du Bois	Comments on land records are provided. County has three Christian Methodist Episcopal congregations. Work states that he has completed his activities associated with the project.
11/5/1908	Ovington to Du Bois	Ovington makes inquiry about Du Bois' sources for the population and crime data that were used in his study on African American quality of life in New York City.[5] Information on the current status of the Lowndes County study is requested.
11/7/1908	Du Bois to Neill	Du Bois requests information concerning the publication date for the Lowndes County study.
11/9/1908	Neill to Du Bois	Neill confirms that the Lowndes County article will be published in the January 1909 edition of the *Bulletin of the Department of Labor*. Du Bois contacts Thorn and Ovington and indicates that the article proofs will be sent to Farnam for review.
12/8/1908	Thorn to Du Bois	Du Bois is invited to speak at the Emancipation meeting to be held at the Calhoun Colored School in Lowndes County on January 1, 1909.

1. M. L. Polean was a disbursement clerk with the Department of Commerce and Labor.
2. James McCall was affiliated with the Alabama Plantation Improvement Society.
3. G. W. Esterly was an auditor with the U.S. Treasury Department.
4. Monroe Work, another first-generation African American male sociologist, was an instructor at the Georgia State Industrial College at the time he completed his duties associated with the Lowndes County study.
5. "The Black North: A Social Study" was a collection of articles by Du Bois that was published in the *New York Times* between November and December 1901. The first article was on the historical development of the quality of life of African Americans in New York City up to 1901. Additional articles addressed African American quality of life in Boston and Philadelphia. The New York City article appeared on November 17, 1901. Five articles were reprinted in book form in 1969 by Arno Press under the title, *The Black North in 1901: A Social Study*.

Table 5.4. *(continued)*

Date	Parties	Communication Topic
1909 (N=1)		
4/22/1909	Du Bois to Farnam	The study manuscript has been with Neill for a year. Du Bois acknowledges that the study is too long and needs to be edited. He is unsure about the study's publication. Du Bois acknowledges that he possesses an incomplete copy of the manuscript that could be forwarded to Farnam.

Source: W. E. B. Du Bois Papers (MS 312), Special Collections and University Archives, University of Massachusetts Amherst Libraries. http://credo.library.umass/.

Bois, 1902a). Three communications took place during 1903 between Du Bois and Walter Wilcox, a chief statistician in the United States Census Office. Wilcox informs Du Bois that he may be able to assist him in requesting the creation of a schedule to collect information on Negro agricultural laborers in Lowndes County (Du Bois, 1903e). Du Bois (1903f) responds indicating that he would like to collect data on the population, sex, age, marital status, literacy, occupational status, land and home ownership, and birthplace of African Americans residing in Lowndes County. Only one correspondence for the project survives for 1904. Here Wright informs Du Bois that the Lowndes County study cannot be authorized in the immediate future (Du Bois, 1904e).

1905

During 1905 Du Bois generated five draft documents outlining various aspects of a proposed social study of African American farmers. The first document is an outline for a social and economic study of a Black Belt county. Here Du Bois (1905c) indicates that demographic data such as population count, sex, age, marital status, birthplace, residence in the county, and educational attainment would be collected for the county's African American population. This venture would be followed by the collection of additional data on housing and families, occupational status, community organizational life, and the general social environment (e.g., laws, disfranchisement, and customs). A faded typed version of this document listing the study variables exists also (Du Bois, 1905d). Many of the topics in the handwritten and typed versions of the study proposal of a Black Belt county were ultimately included in the final version of the 1906 Lowndes County schedule.

The title of the third 1905 document is "Industrial Conditions of the Black Cotton Belt" (Du Bois, 1905e). African American and White Lowndes County cotton farmers were identified specifically as the focus of this project. Du Bois planned to investigate the racial disparities in an agricultural economy where the African American population was more than six times the size of the White population. He wanted to document the wages of African American farmworkers as well as determine the role that women and children played in the farm economy. Labor conditions, land ownership, and migration patterns were to be investigated as well. Du Bois submitted two budget estimates ($1,250 and $750) based on whether 20 or 15 workers with mules being paid either $2.50 or $2.00 a day would be utilized to conduct the house-to-house canvass. The African American and the White populations would be studied, and county land and mortgage records would be searched and copied. The county's laws and administrative organizations would be investigated also (Du Bois, 1905d).

In a fragment of a working draft of a study proposal, Du Bois provided some further details concerning the information to be included in the home schedule. He wanted to collect information on the materials used to build the house, the number and size of the rooms, the primary use of the rooms, and how the rooms were furnished. Additionally, he wanted to be able to provide more details concerning sanitation conditions. The schedules were to be tracked by using an identifying number and name. This would enhance researchers' ability to cross-reference the schedules and check the accuracy of data collected. Finally, the activities of children under age 10 were to be excluded from the data collection (Du Bois, 1905f).

The last document for 1905 is a typed "memoranda" directed to the United States Bureau of Labor. Du Bois is aware that the Bureau wants to conduct a study of a Black Belt county, and he stresses that the study must be empirically based and suggests that Lowndes County would be an appropriate study location for "historical and economic reasons." The Calhoun School could assist with the investigations provided that the school's ties with the project do not harm its reputation in the county. Henry Farnam, a Yale professor and trustee of the Calhoun School, could review the final study report prior to its publication (Du Bois, 1905g).

1906

During this year the Lowndes County, Alabama study is authorized by the Bureau of Labor, now under the direction of Charles Neill. The Calhoun Colored School is utilized as the study's headquarters. A survey schedule is created and data are collected.

The first communication for the year is between Du Bois and Neill and is dated January 19. In this letter Du Bois notes that he visited Lowndes County in December and that he wants to revisit the feasibility of a social study of the county. He argues that a survey-based study could be conducted for $750 to $1,000, that the Calhoun School could assist with the study, and that student canvassers familiar with the county and its residents could collect the requested data (Du Bois, 1906f). Apparently, Du Bois was engaged in service learning one hundred years before it was popularized in colleges and universities. In the surviving Lowndes County study communications, Du Bois refers to the Calhoun Colored School as the Calhoun School. The Calhoun Colored School appears on the school's letterhead.

Working with John Lemon, a staff member at the Calhoun Colored School, Du Bois receives estimates of the costs to canvass the whole county, half the county, and an area that contains 5,000 people in a communication dated January 28. The costs ranged from $550 for the entire county to $91.67 for an area with 5,000 people. The cost for the whole county would include the hiring of ten men and the utilization and care of ten mules for a twenty-day period. Lemon indicated that there were twenty-one precincts in the county (Du Bois, 1906g). On June 22, Lemon provides Du Bois with a revised estimate of the cost to survey the African American and White populations of Lowndes County. The cost is now increased to $1,800. This estimate includes the utilization of twenty men and horses for thirty days. If the cost needs to be lowered, the work could possibly be done for $1,500, but it would be more prudent to assume that the total costs for the project could be as high as $2,000 (Du Bois, 1906h).

Du Bois contacts Neill and indicates that he believes that a reliable study could be completed for $750 to $1,250 minus his cost to prepare the final report. Du Bois stated that to cover the entire county, 6,000 African American families would need to be included in the house-to-house canvass and that a data collector would probably not be able to canvass more than 25 families daily. This would mean that a complete canvass of the county could take 240 days (Du Bois, 1906i). On July 24, G. W. W. Hanger, the acting commissioner of labor, informs Du Bois that Dr. Neill has authorized the Lowndes County study for a total cost of $2,000. Du Bois will be paid $750 to prepare the final report, and the cost associated with collecting the data is set at $1,250. Du Bois accepts the offer (Du Bois, 1906j).

A final document related to 1906 provides some detailed notes concerning the areas to be studied and the data sources. Du Bois may or may not have produced this document. The following Lowndes County data sources are to be consulted: the registry of voters; sheriff's sales and executions; records of the justice of the peace, mayors, and magistrates; teachers' pay for all schools; mortgages and liens for 1900 through 1905; history and records of land ownership since slavery; criminal cases tried from 1886 through 1892; county court docket for 1896 through 1904; poll-tax records from 1899 to 1901; records of votes for all county elections from 1850 to 1906; wills; and finally labor contracts. County officials to be contacted include the probate judge, clerk of court, board of revenue, tax assessors and collectors, county surveyor, sheriff, magistrates, mayors, justices of the peace, local school trustees, the county superintendent of Education, and finally persons at the Board of Education (Du Bois, 1906k).

1907

The largest number of preserved communications related to the Lowndes County, Alabama social study is for 1907. Twenty-four correspondences survive, and several of these communications are discussed in more detail since they provide valuable contextual information about the problems associated with the data tabulations. The data for the house-to-house canvass had been collected and now attention turned to cleaning the data and tabulating the data so that a final report could be produced. The first three communications for the year reference the completion of the data collection, the postage needed to return the schedules to the Bureau of Labor for tabulation, and the return of the corrected schedules (Table 5.4).

In the February 16 communication, Du Bois (1907c) noted that farmers and schoolteachers collected the data for the study, and the codes for basic demographic variables like sex, marital status, place of birth, literacy, and color (i.e., race) were provided. For example, literacy was coded as follows: N = cannot read and write; L = can read and write a letter; and Y = can read and write. Regarding coding discrepancies and issues, Du Bois stated that sometimes "yes" or "no" answers were used for the marital status questions rather than the recommended codes. Also, it appeared that in some instances the birthplace answer was misunderstood, and it is admitted that some of the age data for older persons were not reliable. Additionally, problems were encountered in the coding of the following variables: relatives in the county, occupational status, the collection of household data rather than family data, and housing material. It appeared that the data for acres owned, rented, and cultivated were often confused. Furthermore, the school data were not always clear, and there were some issues involving some of the financial data like rents, mortgages, and liens (Du Bois, 1907c).

Du Bois then informed the Bureau that the following tabulations and cross-tabulations were desired:

- number of households
- sex and age
- birthplace by sex
- race by age
- marital status by age and sex
- literacy by age and sex
- number of children in school, amount of total schooling, and length of school year
- type of home and number of years spent there
- number of rooms in household
- farm size and acreage owned and rented
- farm rent paid with currency or in cotton
- number of farms cross-referenced by the amount of cotton and corn crops rented or owned
- rented or owned farms by farm size and money advanced
- crops by monetary advances
- farm size by debt owed or loan balance
- total balances and debts (Du Bois did not state the nature of the balances or debts)
- money contributed to churches and organizations
- number of deaths by age and sex

The payment of farm rent in cotton was an important variable since cotton was treated the same as currency throughout the South. Du Bois would be able to utilize the requested data to specify the impact the crop lien system had on the local economy. The literacy, age, and sex data could be utilized to document the challenges associated with African American male voter registration, and farm ownership was an important indicator of social mobility (Du Bois, 1907c).

In a correspondence dated February 28, Neill informed Du Bois that the Bureau would only count schedules where the meaning of the response was without question. Neill expressed concerns about being able to address the following data issues: birthplace; persons absent at the time of the survey; frequency in asking the schooling questions; confusion of data for cultivation of acres rented and owned; acres of land occupied versus those under cultivation; accuracy of stock and tools data; crop valuation; interpretation of data related to advances, balances, and debt; and unclear financial contributions data for churches and societies. Since there were many schedules containing ambiguous or questionable answers, Neill recommended that Du Bois come to Washington, DC and work with a Bureau statistician to see if the responses for the questionable schedules could be clarified in a satisfactory manner (Du Bois, 1907d).

Responding to Neill's concerns on March 19, Du Bois (1907e) requested that the schedules be returned to him for editing. He was not concerned about the birthplace discrepancy because a distinction could still be made between persons who were born in Lowndes County and those who were not. Du Bois admitted that it would be difficult to determine the number of family members who were not present in the county at the time the survey was administered, and he argued that all the school-related questions were answered. The acreage question primarily addressed total land and not acreage under cultivation; however, Du Bois did acknowledge that the data related to tools was incomplete. Crop valuations for cotton and corn were based on 1906 market prices, and the debt figures were generally correct. It was noted that many persons who held church membership did not support the church financially. Du Bois included a second typed page and listed financial matters like wages, mortgages, crop liens, and land leases (Du Bois, 1907e). Upon reviewing Du Bois' explanations, Neill advised Du Bois to refrain from including absent family members from the family size measure. It appeared that the most accurate schooling metric was the number of months in school, and Du Bois was advised to drop the tool data from the analysis. Du Bois is invited once more to come to Washington to discuss the data discrepancies with Bureau statisticians (Du Bois, 1907f), and he is reminded in another correspondence that the total costs for the project cannot exceed $2,000 (Du Bois, 1907g).

On May 10, Du Bois received a letter from G. W. W. Hanger, the Acting Commissioner of Commerce and Labor, stating that statistical tables related to the Lowndes County study would not be available before July or August (Du Bois, 1907h). Hanger contacted Du Bois again on August 30 and informed him that Neill had reviewed the Lowndes County schedules and concluded that they contained too many errors. Consequently, all tabulation efforts had been discontinued. Du Bois was asked to move forward with preparing the article for the report and was told that Neill would be willing to meet with him in Washington to determine if there was any way the data collected could be utilized (Du Bois, 1907i).

In a communication dated October 8, Du Bois (1907j) indicated that he went to Washington, DC on September 30, but Neill was not available. He then requests that Neill provide him with the schedules. Du Bois states that the data could be tabulated at Atlanta University and that he would contact persons who could provide the necessary clarifications for some of the data concerns. The reliability of the data would be assumed by Du Bois. Neill responds on November 2 and again maintains that the schedules contain too many errors and indicates that the income and expenditure data are "worthless" (Du Bois, 1907k). The Bureau is unwilling to produce statistical tables. Du Bois is asked to prepare a final report utilizing only data from the schedules that are deemed by the Bureau to be reliable. The schedules will be returned to Du Bois so that he can salvage any statistically reliable information that can be presented in his final report (Du Bois, 1907k).

1908–1909

In the first correspondence of 1908, dated February 6, Du Bois informs Neill that he will submit his Lowndes County article by April 1 (Du Bois, 1908e). This interaction is followed by five exchanges between Du Bois and John Lemon, a staff member at the Calhoun Colored School, whose affiliation with the project ended in May 1908. These communications addressed mortgage payments and a list of churches in the county (Table 5.4). Neither the list of churches nor the data for the four mortgages mentioned have survived. However, a detailed account of the land mortgage payments for Sam Hamilton was provided for the 1897–1905 period in one of the communication exchanges. Mr. Hamilton began with a mortgage balance of $219.68 in 1897. Throughout the period stated annual payments varied from nothing in 1900 to a low payment of $9.03 in 1897 to a large payment of $84.48 in

1903. The last payment, of $22.52 in 1905, resulted in a zero balance (Du Bois, 1908f).

Du Bois submitted his final report on the Lowndes County study in May 1908. He was paid $1,000 for the article. The title of the article was "Negro Labor in Lowndes County, Alabama" (Du Bois, 1908b). On October 1, Monroe Work, a first-generation African American male sociologist who had worked with Du Bois on other projects, informed Du Bois that he had completed all his work related to the Lowndes County project, including a review of the land records for 1902. Mortgages and court dockets for several years were copied, and the existence of three active Colored Methodist Episcopal (CME) churches in Lowndes County was verified. (Note the membership data for the CME churches for 1906 in Table 5.3.) Voter registration books were consulted also (Du Bois, 1908g).

The November 7 exchange between Du Bois and Neill contained an inquiry concerning the publication of the Lowndes County article (Du Bois, 1908h). Neill's reply indicated that the article would appear in the January 1909 issue of the *Bulletin of the Department of Labor* (Du Bois, 1908d). The article did not appear in this issue, and the last available communication related to the Lowndes County study involved an exchange between Du Bois and Farnam dated April 22, 1909. Here Du Bois reminded Farnam that he would be given an opportunity to review the report proofs prior to the study's publication, but he also shared his concern as to whether the Bureau would publish the report. Du Bois acknowledged that the report was too long and needed to be edited and then asked Farnam to request that Neill allow him (Farnam) to review the manuscript on his next visit to Washington. Du Bois mentioned that if a visit was not possible, he could provide Farnam with his "incomplete, but fairly correct copy" of the final report (Du Bois, 1909a).

This sole 1909 communication related to the Lowndes County study is significant because it suggests that, at one point, Du Bois did have an incomplete copy of the manuscript. Perhaps Du Bois sent this draft to Farnam, and it was never returned. The bottom line is, 1) the Bureau never published the report; 2) Du Bois' incomplete draft is not currently available; and 3) the report could have been destroyed, based on Du Bois' statement in his last autobiography (Du Bois, 1968/2007). Thus, was the report destroyed by the Bureau; is it buried in the Bureau's archives, or could Du Bois' incomplete manuscript be in some other location, like Farnam's papers?

CHAPTER 6

The Atlanta Black Church

A Religious Economy Case Study

The Negro's Church (1933), by Benjamin Mays and Joseph Nicholson, is a classic study in the sociology of the Black Church. The study was based on a survey of 185 rural and 609 urban Black churches and utilized data from the 1916 and 1926 *Census of Religious Bodies.* The study was partially replicated by C. Eric Lincoln and Lawrence Mamiya in their 1990 study, *The Black Church in the African American Experience.* Since the United States Census Bureau discontinued its collection of religious data with the publication of the 1936 *Census of Religious Bodies,* Lincoln and Mamiya were unable to utilize religious census data in their study of the Black Church. While the 1980 Glenmary data (Quinn et al., 1982) could have been accessed to provide county-level data on the Black Church, this source would have provided only data for the African Methodist Episcopal Zion Church (AMEZ) and the Christian Methodist Episcopal (CME) Church, two of the seven mainline Black Church denominations. Lincoln and Mamiya did survey 619 rural and 1,531 urban churches between 1978 and 1986 in their attempt to identify major religious participation trends among the mainline Black Church denominations.

Although these two studies represent classic studies in the sociology of the Black Church, W. E. B. Du Bois' *The Negro Church* (1903d/2003), is the first empirically based book-length sociological study of the Black Church (Wortham, 2005a; Zuckerman, Barnes, and Cady, 2003). *The Negro Church* was the formal publication for the eighth Atlanta University Conference on the Study of the Negro Problems. Data sources for Du Bois' edited volume included the 1890 *Census of Religious Bodies,* conference minutes, convention reports, catalogues of theological schools, and special reports from Black and White theological schools, as well as information provided by pastors, officials, school leaders, Black laypersons, and Whites. Data from six different regional case studies of the Black Church were included as well. One case study involved the Black Church in Atlanta. The other five small area Black Church case studies were from two other cities (Richmond and Chicago), a town (Deland, Florida), and two counties (Thomas County, Georgia and Greene County, Ohio).

This case study is particularly interesting for two reasons. First, some of the data for the Atlanta Black Church case study was collected by Du Bois' students in the junior and senior classes at Atlanta University during the 1902–1903 academic year. Second, it provides contemporary researchers with an opportunity to witness Du Bois' use of a triangular methodology, a trademark of his inductive, mixed-methods approach to sociological research. The Atlanta case study included a canvass of 54 mainline Black Churches. The data collected were similar to the type of data provided in the *Census of Religious Bodies* reports and were used to describe major religiosity trends among Black Church denominations. The 1902–1903 Atlanta data provided an interim assessment for the period between the findings for the 1890 and 1906 editions of the *Census of Religious Bodies*. More specific data about the characteristics of individual congregations were provided in fifteen ethnographic descriptions of individual churches and several denominational summaries that were based on fieldwork observations. Also, the religious beliefs of young children were gauged through a survey administered in May 1902 to 1,339 African American children in Atlanta's Black public schools.

THE ATLANTA BLACK CHURCH RELIGIOUS ECONOMY

As noted before, the set of competing religious firms within a specified geographic location constitutes that location's religious economy (Stark, 2007). Sociologists of religion have studied the impact of regulated and deregulated religious economies (i.e., marketplaces) on religious involvement (Finke and Stark, 2000, 2005; Jelen, 2002). The data reported by Du Bois and his students for the 54 Atlanta Black Churches are used here to reconstruct the 1903 Atlanta Black Church religious economy. Thus, what data were collected?

From 1850 to 1936, the United States Census Bureau routinely collected data on such topics as number of churches, church seating capacity, value of church property, church debt, value of parsonages, church membership (total, male, and female), and the number of Sunday schools as well as the number of teachers and members engaged in Sunday school (U.S. Department of Commerce and Labor, 1910; Du Bois, 1903d/2003). In the section of *The Negro Church* devoted to the description of Black Churches in Atlanta, Du Bois (1903d/2003) provided summary statistical data at the denominational level as well as more specific data at the congregational level. These data were patterned after the Religious Bodies Census data.

For example, the general denominational data addressed such topics as number of churches, membership claimed, active membership, value of church property, and church income for 1902. Financial data were specified further according to the following budget expenditure categories: salaries, operating expenses, debt payment, charity–mission work, and denominational support. The mainline Black Church denominations included in the Atlanta study were Baptist Churches (primarily National Baptist Convention), the African Methodist Episcopal Church (AME), and the Colored Methodist Episcopal Church (CME). Data were provided also for four Methodist Episcopal (ME) churches and one church from each of the following denominations: Congregational, Presbyterian, Christian, and Protestant Episcopal. At the individual church level, data were provided on membership claimed, active membership, value of church real estate, and church income.

The 1903 religious adherence rates were calculated based on the membership data that Du Bois provided for the 54 Atlanta Black Churches. Two denominational religious adherence rates are calculated following the format utilized in the Association of Statisticians of American Religious Bodies (ASARB) publications (Grammich et al., 2012). The first denominational religious adherence rate is expressed as the ratio of the denomination's membership to the total Black population. The second denominational religious adherence rate is expressed as the ratio of the denomination's membership to total Black Church membership. The number of churches by denomination, the denominational religious membership data, and the two religious adherence rates for the Atlanta Black Churches in 1903 are displayed in Table 6.1.

The seven traditional mainline Black Church denominations are: African Methodist Episcopal (AME), African Methodist Episcopal Zion (AMEZ), Christian (Colored) Methodist Episcopal (CME), National Baptist Convention, USA Incorporated, National Baptist Convention of America, Unincorporated, Progressive National Baptist Convention, and Church of God in

Table 6.1.   Atlanta Black Church Religious Economy, 1903

	Total Churches		Total Membership	Religious Adherence Rate[1] % of Total	% of Black
Denomination	N	%	Number	Black Population	Church Membership
1. Baptist	29	53.7	10,363	29.0	63.7
2. African Methodist Episcopal	14	25.9	3,242	9.1	19.9
3. Methodist Episcopal	4	7.4	1,333	3.7	8.2
4. Congregational	1	1.9	485	1.4	3.0
5. Colored Methodist Episcopal	3	5.6	440	1.2	2.7
6. Presbyterian	1	1.9	180	0.5	1.1
7. Christian	1	1.9	150	0.4	0.9
8. Protestant Episcopal	1	1.9	68	0.2	0.4
All	54	100.2	16,261	45.5	99.9

1. Calculations are based on data collected by the 1902–1903 Atlanta University sociology undergraduates and a series of denominational tables prepared by Du Bois. The total African American population for the city of Atlanta in 1900 was 35,727 persons (Du Bois 1903d/2003, 69).

Source: Du Bois, *The Negro Church* (1903d/2003).

Christ (Lincoln and Mamiya, 1990). Baptists dominated the 1903 Atlanta Black Church religious economy. Over half of the churches (53.7 percent) were Baptist, while another fourth (25.9 percent) were African Methodist Episcopal. Collectively, the two Black Methodist denominations accounted for thirty percent (31.9 percent) of the Atlanta Black churches, and 85.2 percent of the Black Churches in Atlanta were either Baptist or Methodist (i.e., AME and CME). The remaining congregations represent Black congregations within predominately White denominations.

Du Bois (1903d/2003, 69) noted that the Black population in Atlanta in 1900 was 35,727. Utilizing this figure to calculate the 1903 religious adherence rate based on the ratio of the total Black Church membership to the total African American population, a religious adherence rate of 45.5 percent is generated. Although this figure could be overstated, since the African American population probably increased from 1900 to 1903, it is reasonable to assume that between 40 and 45 percent of African Americans in Atlanta held church membership. Looking within the various denominational groups, Baptists again led the way. Almost three out of every ten African Americans in Atlanta were affiliated with a Baptist church, and one in ten African Americans were affiliated with Black Methodist denominations.

When Atlanta's African American religious adherence rate is expressed as a percent of the Black Church membership, one discovers that essentially two-thirds (63.7 percent) of all African Americans holding church membership were Baptist, and a little more than one in five (22.6 percent) African Americans held membership in either the African Methodist Episcopal Church or the Colored Methodist Episcopal Church. Finally, Baptists and Methodists dominated the Atlanta Black Church religious economy, as essentially seventeen out of every twenty (86.3 percent) African Americans who held church membership were members of one of these two denominations.

In *The Churching of America* (2005), Finke and Stark plot the national trend in religious adherence rates from 1776 to 2005. The adherence rates for 1890 and 1906 are based on data obtained from the *Census of Religious Bodies* reports for those years. From 1890 to 1906, the religious adherence rate for the total population for the United States increased from 45 percent to 51 percent. The 1903 religious adherence rate of 45.5 percent for Atlanta's African American community (Table 6.1) is within the range Finke and Stark report for the general population. The claimed membership and the active membership involvement of Atlanta's African American population in 1903 are presented in Table 6.2. Roughly half (51.8 percent) of African Americans who were members of a congregation were classified as being active participants in religious activities. When the total active membership figure (8,423) is divided by Atlanta's total African American population for 1900 (35,727 persons), between one in five and one in four African Americans (23.6 percent) residing in Atlanta in 1903 were active church members.

Table 6.2.   Atlanta Black Church Average Size and Membership Involvement, 1903

Denomination	Number of Churches	Claimed	Membership Active	% Active	Average Size[1]
1. Baptist	29	10,363	5,274	50.9	357
2. African Methodist Episcopal	14	3,242	1,461	45.1	232
3. Methodist Episcopal	4	1,333	910	68.3	333
4. Congregational	1	485	400	82.5	485
5. Colored Methodist Episcopal	3	440	200	45.5	147
6. Presbyterian	1	180	80	44.4	180
7. Christian	1	150	30	20.0	150
8. Protestant Episcopal	1	68	68[2]	100.0	68
All Denominational Groups	54	16,261	8,423	51.8	301

1. Average size is based on the total membership claimed.

2. This figure is based on the number of communicants stated in the ethnographic description provided for this church. The number of active members was left blank in the "other denominations" statistical table, but Du Bois did include this figure in the active membership data for the general summary table for all denominations (Du Bois, 1903d/2003, 69, 71, 78).

Source: Du Bois, *The Negro Church* (1903d/2003).

Active membership involvement varied among the various denominational groups. The lowest active membership participation rate (20.0 percent) was associated with the lone Christian congregation. Four of the eight denominational groups were in the 44–51 percent range. The 100 percent participation rate for the Protestant Episcopal congregation may be suspect as the number of members for this congregation is the total number of communicants (Du Bois, 1903d/2003). Apparently, Du Bois treated this group as representing the total active membership. This could also reflect a difference in the way denominations record membership and active participation in religious activities. Four out of five (82.5 percent) members of the Congregational church are identified as being active, and two out of three (68.3 percent) members of the Methodist Episcopal churches were recorded as being active. In terms of absolute numbers, total membership "claimed" and "active" was greatest among the Baptist congregations. However, only one out of two (50.9 percent) Baptists were identified as being active members.

As organizations grow, certain internal dynamics begin to change. It often becomes harder for larger groups to reach a consensus. Interrelationships among members as well as the ties among members and organizational leaders may become less frequent and more formal. As social ties weaken, absenteeism may increase (Johnstone, 2016). Given this scenario, it is hypothesized that *active participation in a religious organization is inversely proportional to organizational size*. The average size of the 54 congregations included in the 1903 Atlanta Black Church study was 301 members, of which half (51.8 percent) were active. Average church size ranged from a low of 68 members for the single Protestant Episcopal congregation to a high of 485 for the single Congregational church. However, when one looks at the number of churches and the number of total members and active members for the two largest groups, one observes that, compared to the African Methodist Episcopal churches, the Baptist churches were larger and had a higher percentage of active members (Table 6.2). This is the exact opposite of what was hypothesized. Removing the Protestant Episcopal congregation from the analysis since its percentage of active membership is suspect, the bivariate correlation between the percent active membership and average church size for the remaining seven denominational groups is strong, positive, and statistically significant ($r = 0.864$; $p = 0.012$). Again, the hypothesis is rejected. Among the 54 Black Churches included in the 1903 Atlanta Black Church religious economy, active organizational participation increases as group size increases. This finding is consistent with Du Bois' claim that the

Black Church was the educational, political, and religious center of African American life (Du Bois, 1899a/1996, 1903b/2007, 1903d/2003). The church functioned as a support network for a community whose members were living in a world where racial prejudice and discrimination were common occurrences.

Additionally, Du Bois provided detailed statistics with regard to church finances. Budget expenditures by major denominational groups are presented in Table 6.3. The five expenditure categories are salaries, operating expenses, debt, charities, and denominational support. Expenditures for the two largest denominational groups, Baptists and Methodists, are compared, and the single Congregational, Presbyterian, Christian, and Protestant Episcopal congregations are included in the "Other Churches" category. No financial data were provided for the Presbyterian church.

Churches in the Other Churches category allocated over half (53.0 percent) of their budget to salaries. It is assumed that this category is primarily pastoral salaries (Table 6.4). Average church salaries were lowest among the Baptist churches, where average annual church salaries were $372.79. This figure was 85 percent of the average salaries for Methodist churches and only 47 percent of the average salaries for Other Churches. Salaries

Table 6.3. Atlanta Black Church Budget Expenditures by Denomination, 1903

	Denominational Group					
	Baptist Churches (N = 29)		Methodist Churches (N = 21)[1]		Other Churches (N = 3)[2]	
Expenditure Category	Amount	%	Amount	%	Amount	%
1. Salaries	$10,811.00	46.5	$9,174.53	39.7	$2,394.00	53.0
Average Church Salary	372.79		436.88		798.00	
2. Operating Expenses	4,629.70	19.9	3,585.75	15.5	1,176.91	26.1
Average Church Expenses	159.64		170.75		392.30	
3. Debt and Interest	4,493.40	19.3	7,510.02	32.5	539.08	11.9
Average Church Debt/Interest	154.94		357.62		179.69	
4. Charities	2,751.60	11.8	1,137.50	4.9	380.80	8.4
Average Church Charities	94.88		54.17		126.93	
5. Denominational Support	573.60	2.5	1,694.00	7.3	25.00	0.6
Average Church Support	19.78		80.67		8.33	
Total Denominational Expenses	$23,259.30	100.0	$23,101.80	99.9	$4,515.79	100.0
Average Church Expenses	802.03		1,100.09		1,505.25	

1. Methodist Churches include African Methodist Episcopal, Colored Methodist Episcopal, and Methodist Episcopal. The first two denominations are mainline Black Church denominations.

2. Other Churches include: Congregational, Episcopal, and Christian. Data for the lone Presbyterian church were not available.

Source: Du Bois, *The Negro Church* (1903d/2003).

Table 6.4.   Atlanta Black Church Ministers' Salaries, 1903

| | Ministerial Group | | | |
| | All Ministers | | Fixed Salaries | |
Annual Salary Range	Number	%	Number	%
$1,000 or more	7	13.0	7	15.2
$750–$999	3	5.6	3	6.5
$500–$749	10	18.5	10	21.7
$300–$499	7	13.0	7	15.2
$100–$299	8	14.8	8	17.4
$50–$99	6	11.1	6	13.0
$49 and under	5	9.3	5	10.9
No fixed salary	8	14.8	—	—
Total	54	100.1	46	99.9

Source: Du Bois, The Negro Church (1903d/2003).

represented the largest expense category for all three denominational group categories. Baptists allocated similar proportional amounts of their budgets to covering normal operating expenses (19.9 percent) and debt and interest (19.3 percent). Operating expenses was the second-largest expense category for the Other Churches. However, the Methodist congregations were allocating one-third (32.5 percent) of their budgets to debt retirement, and the third major expense was operating expenses (15.5 percent). The average debt expenditure for a Methodist church ($357.62) was significantly higher than the same average expenditure for a church in the Other Churches ($179.69) and the Baptist ($154.94) categories. While Baptists collectively allocated a larger proportion of their budget expenditures to charity work (11.8 percent) compared to the Other Churches (8.4 percent) and the Methodists (4.9 percent), the average amount sent to charities was highest among the Other Churches ($126.93) compared to the amounts recorded for the Baptist ($94.88) and Methodist ($54.17) congregations. Finally, Methodist churches directed more financial resources toward denominational support (7.3 percent). Denominational support was the smallest budget item for the Baptist churches and the Other Churches.

Du Bois (1903d/2003) provided a glimpse of the distribution of salaries among ministers serving the 54 Black Churches included in the study. The salary ranges are displayed in Table 6.4. Only one in seven ministers (14.8 percent) did not have a fixed salary. The income differences among ministers with fixed salaries were pronounced. A little more than four in ten ministers (43.4 percent) received an annual salary of $500 or more, while a similar percentage of ministers (45.6 percent) received an annual income from $50 to $499. Among the ministers reporting a fixed salary, 10.9 percent received an annual salary of $49 or less.

ETHNOGRAPHIC DESCRIPTIONS OF ATLANTA BLACK CHURCHES

The data obtained from the student-led canvass of the Black Churches in Atlanta were utilized to specify the denominational distribution of churches, identify denominational market shares, document affiliation and active involvement levels, and highlight major expense categories as well as the distribution of pastor salaries. Additional information about the nature of pastoral leadership, membership characteristics, and community impact was provided in the ethnographic summaries included in the discussion of Atlanta's Black Churches (Du Bois, 1903d/2003, 72–79).

Baptists

The Baptist churches were grouped based on their size and available financial resources. The educational level of the pastors and members of the smaller churches was identified as low, and many of the church buildings were described as being in poor condition and located in less affluent locations. The larger churches attracted a broader cross-section of persons from the African American community. Several of these churches were described as being among the most affluent and influential in the area. The congregational style of church governance was noted also. Baptists often refer to this leadership style as the "priesthood of believers."

More detailed descriptions were included for five Baptist churches and one Primitive Baptist church. The minister of the Primitive Baptist church was portrayed as being a person of good moral standing who possessed limited formal education. Primitive Baptists prefer that their ministers support themselves by being bi-vocational; however, conflict existed in this congregation because the current minister refused to seek outside employment. The congregation included many older members with limited formal education. The congregation met once a month in a wooden building, and its major purpose was serving the needs of its members. The group's community impact was perceived as being minimal.

The active memberships of the three small Baptist congregations ranged from six members to twenty-five members. These congregations are described now, from smallest to largest. The smallest church met in a small rooming house, and there was some doubt as to the moral character of the pastor and the membership. The second small church had experienced some pastoral leadership change, and the congregation did not offer regular Bible study (i.e., Sunday school). This congregation was involved in a very limited amount of charitable work. The minister of the third congregation was bi-vocational (a pastor and a tailor), had some college training, and was identified as a moral person. The members were described as being dedicated, but the neighborhood location was perceived as undesirable. Consequently, the members were considering relocating the church.

The minister of one of the larger Baptist congregations was a good speaker, but his moral character was questioned. The general character of the membership was questioned also even though this congregation had an active women's mission group, who were engaged in community ministry. On the other hand, the other large Baptist church had 1,560 active members. The minister was highly educated and respected. The church appealed primarily to persons from the middle and upper classes and included many businessmen, property owners, and skilled laborers. The church carried no outstanding debt, supported two mission ventures, and operated the largest Sunday school program in Georgia.

Methodists

Like the Baptist churches, the Methodist churches were distinguished on the basis of membership size. As was the case with the Baptist churches, the larger Methodist churches attracted more business professionals and skilled workers. In contrast to the Baptist churches, the Methodist churches carried more debt. This finding was confirmed earlier by the empirical data obtained from the statistical canvass (Table 6.3). The Methodist congregations were described as being involved in some charitable ministries, and the ministers were characterized as possessing sound morals and being reasonably educated. Several of the ministers had seminary training.

More detailed ethnographic descriptions were provided for the three African Methodist Episcopal (AME) churches, the two Methodist Episcopal (ME) churches, and a Christian [Colored] Methodist Episcopal (CME) church. The smallest AME church had eighty-five active members and was led by a pastor serving two other congregations. In ministry circles this is referred to as serving a "two-point charge." The congregation was described as being poor. The church was adjacent to a cemetery, and many White residences were nearby. The other small AME church had recently experienced a schism, which appeared to be along class lines. Those who left this congregation formed the Christian Church that is included in the Atlanta Black Church canvass. The large AME congregation included 600 active members, and persons representing different age groups, occupations, and social classes were attracted to this church. The new worship building reflected the church's affluence. The building materials included granite and yellow pine, and the church was equipped with a pipe organ, electric light fixtures, and theater-style seating.

One small and one large ME congregation were included in the ethnographic descriptions of individual Methodist churches. The smaller church was portrayed as having some influence in the community. Charitable work was conducted by the Women's Home Missionary Society and the Epworth League. Many of the members who attended the church worked as laborers for the railroad. The minister was a seminary graduate and was revered by the congregation. The minister of the larger ME congregation was highly respected, and the membership was better educated. The church was involved in charitable work and attracted young people. As part of its educational ministry, the church offered classes in cooking, sewing, and religious growth and development.

The CME congregation had only fifty active members, but they did build the present brick church building. The church began in a one-room cabin and had moved seven different times. The pastors of this congregation had received formal educational training but were described as being loud. This may have been a reference to the emotionalism that characterized some Black Church traditions, particularly in the South (Du Bois, 1903d/2003; Lincoln and Mamiya, 1990; Baer and Singer, 1992; Johnstone, 2016).

Other Churches

The pastors of the Congregational, Protestant Episcopal, and Presbyterian churches in the study were well educated and of the highest moral standing. One minister was a Fisk graduate while another had earned a degree from Yale. The members of these three congregations were described as possessing a high school education. The members displayed sound moral character, and professional men and women were drawn to these congregations. The worship style was less emotional.

The character of the Protestant Episcopal and Congregational ministers was described as exemplary; the character of the Christian church's pastor was questioned. The members of the Protestant Episcopal Church were drawn largely from the middle class, and the church was not very involved in benevolent work. The Christian church, which had been formed as a result of a schism, was experiencing financial problems. The Protestant Episcopal and the Congregational congregations maintained a strong community presence. The Protestant Episcopal church supported a school that served 120 students, and the Congregational church maintained a mission in one of the Atlanta slums. The educational attainment level of the members of the Congregational church was the highest of the 54 Atlanta Black Churches included in this case study. This church benefited from being located in an affluent area and did not carry any debt.

The ethnographic descriptions provided in the Atlanta Black Church case study reveal that some of the ministers were fairly well trained while others were not. Members were drawn from all social classes. A few of the churches had a strong community presence, but it appears that most of the churches, for which ethnographic summaries were provided, did not.

Throughout the ethnographic section of the Atlanta Black Church case study, Du Bois (1903d/2003) reflected on the evolution of the Black Church. He maintained that two Black Church traditions had emerged since slavery. One tradition was characterized by congregations led by a strong, authoritative, motivating personality. This leadership style appears to exemplify what Weber (1904–1905, 1920/1996; 1922/1964) identified as "charismatic authority." In a second Black Church tradition, churches adopted a more democratic governing structure. Du Bois viewed the first tradition as giving way to the second tradition as he described the emergence of ministers who were logical thinkers, who possessed strong organizational skills, and who were able to raise money. Today, these last three roles are seen as primary roles assumed by clergy (Johnstone, 2016).

The reference to the more deliberate manner of many of the Atlanta Black Church pastors may be taken as an indicator of a move away from the emotionalism that had characterized some forms of worship within the Black Church tradition. The following description of one of the more emotional Black Church services was provided by a student attending a large Baptist church.

He [the minister] began by telling the history of the Knights of Pythias. This was interesting and I could understand him; but when he shut the Bible and began to preach I could not understand him at first. As soon as I could distinguish between the words and the peculiar sound made by the intaking of his breath, I found myself listening to what the people called "a good sermont." During his talk he spit behind the altar many times, and often raised his voice to a veritable yell. I could not keep any record of his exact words. (Du Bois, 1903d/2003, 76)

Following the description of the student's experience, Du Bois offered this commentary: "Such churches grow into large and influential organizations, losing many of their unconventional features and becoming very much like churches in any part of the land." In this statement one can see where Du Bois had anticipated the ideas stated later by Weber (1904–1905, 1920/1996; 1922/1964) in his church-sect typology and by Niebuhr (1929) in his church-sect theory. Weber maintained that emotionalism and mystical beliefs characterized sects, whereas churches intellectualized their teachings. Likewise, Niebuhr argued that sects maintain an otherworldly focus while churches concentrate on current experiences. Over time the religious groups that persist maintain a more "this world" focus. In other words, sects become churches (Stark, 2007). Finke and Stark (2005) utilized this framework to describe the rise of Baptists and Methodists from "upstart sects" to established, mainline churches. In *The Negro Church*, Du Bois (1903d/2003) appeared to be describing a similar transformation within the Black Church.

A CHRISTIAN BELIEFS SURVEY

During May 1902, Du Bois (1903d/2003) administered a survey on Christian beliefs to 1,339 African American children attending Atlanta's Black public schools. This survey is among the earliest sociological surveys of children's religious beliefs in the U.S. The students surveyed were aged 7 to 18. Since Du Bois did not indicate which schools were surveyed or how the participants were selected, the representative nature of the survey is questioned. However, the survey may be treated as an exploratory study that was based on a convenience sample (Babbie, 2016).

The students were asked five questions. The first question addressed whether or not a student identified as a Christian. The next three questions concerned the students' church participation, their desire to attend church, and their reason for attending a particular church. The fifth question addressed the children's understanding of what it means to be a Christian. Du Bois (1903d/2003) provided the raw frequencies for all the response categories associated with each question by age level in the section of *The Negro Church* titled "Children and the Church." In a concluding raw frequency table addressing what being a Christian meant, four summary categories were presented and the responses of younger children (aged 7–12) and older children (aged 13–18) were compared.

This younger–older children comparison is adopted in a reconstruction of the survey findings presented in Table 6.5. Rather than showing only the raw frequencies for each response category by every age level, percentage responses for three age categories are compared. These age categories include: 1) all children (aged 7–18), 2) younger children (aged 7–12), and 3) older children (aged 13–18). The total number of responses for each question is reported also. While the answers to the first and last questions either equal or roughly approximate the sample size (N = 1,339), the answers to questions three and four exceeded the number of survey participants. These discrepancies may be due to double counting and misclassification of data by age. The total response to the second question is understated by 45 cases. For this question, the age of the respondent in several instances was not stated.

A little more than a third (36.9 percent) of all the children surveyed indicated that they were Christians. The older children were more likely to state that they were Christian and were almost evenly divided with respect to whether or not they considered themselves to be a Christian (i.e., 46.0 percent responded "yes" and 54.0 percent responded "no"). The percentage difference (delta, Δ) in the "yes" and "no" responses between the younger and older age groups is statistically significant. Riordan and Mazur (1988) maintain that a 10-percentage point response spread in survey data may be taken as reflecting a difference large enough to be treated as statistically significant.

Essentially, nineteen out of twenty children in all the age categories indicated that they went to church and liked going to church. When the children were asked why they liked a certain church, the most popular response was "because of parents or relatives" (54.7 percent). The younger children–older children percentage difference related to this particular response was not statistically significant but could be treated as approaching statistical

Table 6.5. Survey of Christian Beliefs among African American Children Ages 7–18 in Atlanta's Black Public Schools: 1902 (N = 1,339)

Question/Response	Age Group		
	Ages 7–18 Percent	Ages 7–12 Percent	Ages 13–18 Percent
1. Are you a Christian?			
Yes	36.9	29.0	46.0[1]
No	63.1	71.0	54.0[1]
Number of responses	1,339	720	619
2. Do you go to church?			
Yes	95.5	93.9	97.4
No	2.5	4.1	0.9
Sometimes	1.9	2.0	1.7
Do not know	0.2	0.0	0.0
Number of responses	1,294	639	653
3. Do you like to go to church?			
Yes	97.8	96.8	98.9
No	1.4	2.2	0.5
Sometimes	0.1	0.0	0.2
Do not know	0.8	1.1	0.5
Number of responses[2]	1,393	740	653
4. Why do you like a certain church best?			
Because of parents or relatives[3]	54.7	59.3	49.4
I go there	9.4	8.5	10.4
I believe in that denomination	7.7	4.6	11.1
I am a member	5.7	3.8	7.9
It helps me	2.8	4.3	1.1
Miscellaneous[4]	9.7	7.9	11.8
Do not know	10.1	11.5	8.4
Number of responses[2]	1,383	737	646
5. What does it mean to be a Christian?			
Mystical, figurative, and theological statements[1,5]	40.0	28.4	53.5
Moral goodness[1]	21.9	26.9	16.1
Church service	15.8	17.8	13.5
Love of persons	4.6	4.3	4.9
Goodness and love for Jesus	4.4	8.1	0.2
Baptism	2.6	2.4	2.8
Obey the ten commandments	2.4	2.1	2.8
Do not know	2.7	3.6	1.6
Unanswered	5.6	6.3	4.7
Number of responses	1,329	714	615

1. The percentage difference between the two age groups is statistically significant.

2. According to Du Bois, the survey was administered to 1,339 children ages 7–18 attending Atlanta's Black public schools in May 1902. The total number of responses exceeded this number for questions 3 and 5. This may be due to double counting and/or misclassification of data by age.

3. The percentage difference between the two age groups approaches statistical significance ($\Delta = 9.9 < 10.0$).

4. The Miscellaneous category includes such responses as: "I have never attended any others"; "they treat me nicely there"; "I think Christ was of that denomination"; "it is a good, nice church, or very large"; "they have good services"; "it has the best method"; "my girl goes there"; "the people are good"; "I was converted there"; and "I can do more good there" (Du Bois, 1903d/2003, 186).

5. This category includes such expressions as: "Child of God"; "soldiers of Christ"; "sins forgiven"; "to be born again"; and "to keep the faith" (Du Bois, 1903d/2003,188). The age-group percentage difference is statistically significant.

Source: Du Bois, *The Negro Church* (1903d/2003).

significance ($\Delta = 9.9 < 10.0$ percentage points). Younger children were more likely to state that they liked a particular church because of their parents or relatives. These data provide some support for the "family cycle theory of church participation," which suggests that parents tend to value their children being exposed to religious instruction and are more likely to take their younger children to church (Roof and Johnson, 1993; Roof, 1993). On the other hand, almost one in ten children indicated that they did not know why they liked a particular church.

In his analysis of the raw frequency responses for the younger children versus the older children as related to their understanding of being a Christian, Du Bois (1903d/2003, 189) concluded that younger children tended to equate being a Christian with moral goodness while older children associated being a Christian with conforming to "a higher will" or "to be born again." The current analysis reveals that the age-group percentage difference for each of these first two perspectives is statistically significant. This finding is consistent with Elkind's religious identity developmental model. Elkind maintains that younger children (ages 8–9) conceptualize their religious identity in more concrete terms, like goodness; whereas older children (ages 10–12) move more toward abstract conceptualizations, like "being born again" (Johnstone, 2016). Fowler (1981) outlines a similar pattern in his "stages of faith development" model. During the early school-age years, children view their religious encounters in more literal terms. When adolescence is attained, children begin to evaluate their developing religious beliefs against those held by their parents or other family members. Finally, the African American children attending Atlanta's Black public schools expressed some awareness of a conceptual link between religious beliefs and practices. One in six children equated Christianity with engaging in church-related activities (i.e., church service).

CONCLUSION

Du Bois was able to provide a more detailed, nuanced description of the 1903 Atlanta Black Church religious economy by collecting and integrating ethnographic and survey data. Employing a triangular methodology, he specified the major players in Atlanta's Black Church religious economy and identified membership patterns, involvement levels, congregational expenditures, and children's religiosity patterns. The ethnographic data provided valuable insights into the quality of pastoral leadership, audiences attracted to certain congregations, and congregational involvement in community activities.

The Atlanta Black Church case study represents one of the earliest empirical small area social studies of a religious group in the United States. The involvement of students in the data collection process suggests that Du Bois should be included among the pioneers of the "service learning" movement. Furthermore, Du Bois is one of the founding figures in congregational studies. The data included in the Atlanta case study is typical of the information that is often gleaned in current congregational analyses (Woolever and Bruce, 2010).

CHAPTER 7

Prayer as Social Commentary
in Prayers for Dark People

W. E. B. Du Bois attended a Congregationalist church with his mother with some degree of regularity when he was growing up in Great Barrington, Massachusetts, but his later stance on organized religion has been an issue of debate among scholars. Zuckerman (2009) speaks of Du Bois as irreligious, Blum (2007) portrays him as an American prophet, and Kahn (2009) describes his pragmatic "divine discontent." Given Du Bois' disdain for religious dogma and religious orthodoxy (1897b, 1968/2007), Johnson (2008) argues that Du Bois was more of an agnostic. Although Du Bois later embraced Marxism and did not subscribe to an anthropomorphic view of the supernatural, he did utilize religious imagery in addressing social injustice and believed that religious organizations could promote social reform (Du Bois, 1903d/2003, 1920/2007, 1968/2007).

Perhaps it would be more accurate to speak of Du Bois' "dialectical" approach to religion. Aware of a contradiction between expressed religious beliefs and actual practices, Du Bois held this contradiction in tension. He could view the "sorrow songs" as authentic expressions of the African American experience (Du Bois, 1903b/2007) and portray the Black Church as an integrative mechanism (Du Bois, 1899a/1996). At the same time, he could be critical of Black Church leadership and the church's failure to provide moral guidance and address the African American community's social and economic needs (Du Bois, 1903d/2003; Du Bois and Dill, 1914/2010).

This religious dialectic is presented in *Prayers for Dark People*. Edited and first published posthumously in 1980 by Herbert Aptheker, this little-known volume includes seventy-one prayers that appear to have been composed by Du Bois for Atlanta University students between January 1909 and May 1910. Since Du Bois left Atlanta University in July 1910, this volume of prayers helps document his empirical sociologist–public sociologist transition. Seeking to highlight the role that character would play in addressing the injustices African American children and young adults would face in a world dominated by the color line these prayers functioned as social commentary on "the Negro problems."

THE SOCIAL CONTEXT OF *PRAYERS FOR DARK PEOPLE*

Had Du Bois not given Herbert Aptheker an envelope labeled "prayers" just prior to his leaving the United States for Ghana in 1961, these prayers may have remained unknown and unpublished. Most of the seventy-one prayers were handwritten on scraps of paper, and only ten were given titles. A framing date for these prayers on the front end may be supplied by the reference to Edgar Allan Poe's birthday one hundred years earlier in a prayer apparently intended for January 19, 1909. "May 3, 1910" is written on the back of another prayer and may function as the back end of the dating period (Aptheker, 1980). It is possible that some of the prayers were written earlier or later than the timeline proposed.

In an earlier study on the history of Atlanta University, Du Bois (1905b) stressed that the school functioned as each student's home. This point is referenced in several of the prayers. Each dormitory was supervised by a woman who served as a surrogate mother, and teachers and students shared meals together. Atlanta University provided a rare environment within the Jim Crow South where African Americans and Whites interacted socially. Students received religious and moral instruction and were encouraged to develop effective study habits and practice good hygiene.

While Du Bois had utilized the sorrow songs to capture the essence of the African American experience in *The Souls of Black Folk* (1903b/2007), the prayers written for the Atlanta University students were a vehicle that allowed Du Bois to highlight character qualities that, as the students matured, they would need to promote social change and enhance social mobility. For Du Bois, religious songs and prayers were ritual forms that could be utilized to evoke collective experiences and to address racial inequality. While the power of religious rituals is articulated clearly in Durkheim's *The Elementary Forms of the Religious Life* (1912/1995), Du Bois was equally aware of how ritual practices could capture and reflect social conditions and have the power to shape social consciousness and social structures. Perhaps Durkheim's understanding of the "totemic principle" was not all that new within the sociology of religion, a developing sociological subfield. So how did Du Bois specifically use prayers to reflect social reality and stimulate social action?

THE STRUCTURE OF *PRAYERS FOR DARK PEOPLE*

Aptheker begins his reconstructed volume of Du Bois' prayers with what was apparently Du Bois' working list of prayer topics (Table 7.1). The list addressed some of the pressing social issues of the day. Du Bois composed prayers addressing ten of the sixteen topics identified in this list. These topics were war (and peace), poverty, orphans, cripples, children, charity, criminals, women's rights (rather than women's suffrage), labor wars (rather than trade unions), and old age.

Du Bois (1898a) was committed to confronting the social issues impacting the African American community. Through the prayers offered to the Atlanta University students, perhaps he was trying to instill a social conscience, a sense of social responsibility, and a thirst for social justice. While Du Bois did not compose prayers on sickness, insanity, miners, tuberculosis, science, and art, he had addressed many of these topics in his earlier sociological writings. For instance, poverty, sickness, tuberculosis, children,

Table 7.1. Prayer Topics Listed in *Prayers for Dark People*

* War (and Peace)[1]
* Poverty
* Orphans (Homeless)
* Cripples
Sick
Insane
Toilers in Mines
Tuberculosis
* Children
* Charity
* Criminals (Theft)
* Trade Unions (Labor Wars)
* Women's Suffrage (Women's Rights)
* Old Age
Science
Art

1. Topics identified by an asterisk (*) were the subject of a specific prayer. The topics in parentheses represent a related prayer subject addressed by Du Bois.

criminals, trade unions, and suffrage were discussed in *The Philadelphia Negro* (1899a/1996) and in several of the Atlanta University Conference annual reports (e.g., *The Negro Artisan*, 1902b; *Some Notes on Crime Particularly in Georgia*, 1904d; *The Health and Physique of the Negro American*, 1906c; and *The Negro American Family*, 1908a). Furthermore, orphans, cripples, the sick, children, charity, criminals, and old age were addressed after Du Bois formally left Atlanta University in *Morals and Manners among Negro Americans* (Du Bois and Dill, 1914/ 2010), a conference annual report coedited with Augustus Dill. Since several of the topics in Du Bois' beginning prayer list were never addressed, perhaps the 1980 volume edited by Aptheker is a fragment of an unfinished work that was eventually abandoned. This is probable; after leaving Atlanta University in July 1910, Du Bois was employed as the director of publications for the NAACP and was the editor of the organization's major publication, *The Crisis*.

Following Du Bois' working list, Aptheker presents the seventy-one prayers. The prayer numbers referenced in this study have been supplied by the author but follow the sequence of prayers provided by Aptheker. The first fifty-eight prayers do not have titles. These prayers are Christian and often begin with a reference to the deity as "God" or "Lord." Many of the prayers are short (ten to fifteen lines) and conclude with "Amen" and a reference to an Old Testament or New Testament scripture. The next twelve prayers (Prayers 59–70) have titles and beginning with Prayer 60 are numbered 1 through 10. Their titles are as follows: Work, Christmas, New Year, Reverence, Lies, Courtesy, Strength, Ambition, Persistence, Promptness, and Cleanliness. The title for the prayer on promptness was supplied by Aptheker, and Du Bois did not provide a number for the prayer on cleanliness (Aptheker, 1980). Du Bois' emphasis on building character as a mechanism to be employed when facing and confronting the challenges of a world divided by the color line is highlighted in nine of these twelve prayers. Two of the remaining prayers focus on the meaning and purpose of specific holidays (Christmas and New Year's Day), and the collection concludes with an untitled prayer on the value of money (Prayer 71).

In Prayer 71, Du Bois encouraged students to learn to appreciate money's real value as well as the sacrifices people make on their behalf so that they may have a good life. Du Bois then went on to associate time with money, work, and life. These young students were then reminded not to waste either money or life. At the end of the prayer, verses 4, 7–8, 11, 18, and 22–23 from Proverbs 13 were referenced to reinforce the prayer's main tenets. Du Bois probably utilized the King James Version (KJV) of the Bible, also known as the Authorized Version, given his use of Victorian prose in many of his writings, such as in his 1911 novel, *The Quest of the Silver Fleece*. Although Du Bois (1968/2007) rarely attended organized religious services following his Harvard and Berlin years, his use of religious themes was demonstrated in the essay "The Sorrow Songs," included in *The Souls of Black Folk* (1903b/2007), in poems like "Credo" and "A Litany at Atlanta," which were originally published in 1904 and 1906, and in this posthumously published collection of prayers.

Prayer 71 also showcases Du Bois' stance on the value of work, waste, materialism, gratitude, and the significance of a family's financial sacrifices for their children. Du Bois was known for his strong work ethic (D. Lewis, 2009). Perhaps the reference to "the mother's heart" is based on Du Bois' (1968/2007) memories of his mother's sacrifices, dedication, and commitment to provide for him. Furthermore, the themes presented in this prayer reflect the basic tenets of the "economic ethic of the Black Church" (Lincoln and Mamiya, 1990). This economic ethic underscored the value of getting an education, securing a job, taking care of one's family, and saving for a rainy day.

Based on a close reading of the seventy-one prayers, a summary table has been created to showcase the primary theme of each prayer by identifying key phrases and images presented in each prayer. The results of this analysis are presented in Table 7.2. Some of the prayers address holidays like Thanksgiving, Christmas, the New Year, and Easter. Several of the prayers were appeals to students to take their work seriously. Hard work and the building of character were seen as necessary if one were to address the inequalities and injustices of a society structured on the basis of race.

Returning to the structure of the prayers, a scripture reference was placed at the bottom of fifty-six of the seventy-one prayers. The various scripture references are presented in Table 7.3. Each scripture reference is followed by the prayer number and the prayer theme/title. No scripture reference was provided for fifteen prayers. There were thirty-seven references to Old Testament passages and twenty-three references to New Testament passages. Ten of the thirty-seven Old Testament references address one of the Psalms, and Genesis, 1 Samuel, Ecclesiastes, and Isaiah are each referenced four times. Fifteen of the twenty-three New Testament references were drawn from one of the four gospels (i.e., Matthew, Mark, Luke, and John). Luke is cited six times, and Matthew and John are referenced four

Table 7.2. Themes, Key Phrases, and Images for Prayers in *Prayers for Dark People*

Prayer Number	Theme	Key Phrases and Images
1.	New Year's Resolution (January 1909?)	Action, deliverance from sloth, courage to fail, and never cease striving.
2.	The Curse of Drinking (January 19, 1909)	Our national weakness and slavery of drink.
3.	Peace	Save this government, strength, honesty, courage, and all men are free and equal.
4.	Springtime	Work is heavy, wearisome toil, uplift our hearts, things worthwhile, and Thy peace.
5.	The Reaping of Deeds	Veiled and mighty harvest; ease of Evil now.
6.	Salvaging the Good	Faulty thinking, neglected education of a child, ignorance in youth, good from bad, and these last days.
7.	Commencement (June 1909?)	Threshold of the elect; chosen souls; knowledge; and culture.
8.	Play and Recreation	Seriousness of play, mistaken play, work and rest, waste of energy, and debauchery.
9.	Summer Freedom	License, selfishness and irregularity, prisoned in ignorance, renewed service to Goodness & Beauty.
10.	Thanksgiving	Health and strength; sun, rain, and peace; seize the day; possibilities, gratitude, and appreciation.
11.	Joy of Giving (Advent?)	Happy friends are a gift from God; gift of service.
12.	Advent Season	Spirit of Peace and Joy, goodwill toward men, spirit of home, and protection from drunkenness.
13.	Christmas	The Christ spirit reborn in homes and country; selfishness, languor, and envy versus humility, poverty and sacrifice; needless warships.
14.	Confidence in New Year (January 1910?)	Self-confidence, power, and purpose; lack of faith; hesitancy; do what we wish; and faith and works.
15.	Persistence and Endurance	Listlessness and shirking; rest before rest is earned; and strength and knowledge.
16.	Persistence in Work Begun	Strength of body and mind, determination, doubts of friends and enemies, distrust of self, death of winter, resurrection of spring, and good from evil.
17.	Personal Betterment	Honesty and strength to face faults; justice; goodness; and efficiency.
18.	Immortality	Shadow of death to human blindness; brightness of newer greater life.

Table 7.2. *(Continued)*

Prayer Number	Theme	Key Phrases and Images
19.	Mighty Causes	Dare to do the deed; freeing of women; training of children; hate and murder; poverty, work, sacrifice; death; and the spirit of Esther.
20.	The Struggle for Freedom	Better government and free institutions; brothers and sisters (Persia, China, Russia, Turkey, Africa, and America); and war and caste.
21.	Honor	Honor of home, school, race, and Thy name; willingness to do lowly deeds; sacrifice; and achievements that benefit others.
22.	The Gift of Charity	Value of people, rash judgments, and humility.
23.	The Gift of Death	The rest that is Peace; the legacy of an old man; sacrifice, honesty, and goodness; Kingdom of Heaven among men.
24.	Our Global Kin	All those in bonds: lowly, wretched, ignorant, and weak; our problems and the world's problems; and responsibility and strength.
25.	Endurance	Learn to finish things, fulfill the promise, temptation of shirking, and grit to endure.
26.	True Education	The unpleasant task, the hard lesson, the bitter experience, path to knowledge, and power and good.
27.	Sins of Labor Wars	The great battle for bread; strike, turmoil, and litigation; do justly, love mercy, and walk humbly; extravagance, generosity, and the face of poverty.
28.	Worthy Work	Desire to know, learn, and do; host of witnesses; and worthy of heritage.
29.	Simple Beauty	Reverence the great and minute, strive for the good and true, and still small voice of duty.
30.	Truth and Ignorance	Thou light of the world; persons more ignorant than wicked; light to see, learn, and know; and those that sit in darkness.
31.	Dedicated Students	Religion expressed in work, honesty of endeavor, thoroughness, singleness, and purity of purpose; and unforgivable sin/blasphemy–waste time and opportunity.
32.	Being Useful Instruments	Helping, cheering, and doing; happiness of human souls; service; secret treasures; and lesson of life.
33.	Better Government	Responsibility of leaders; private gain versus greater good; disfranchised duty–preparation, observation, and intelligent criticism; and civilized Christian state.
34.	Success Now	Study now; seed time; later harvest and playtime; and work, study, and success.

Table 7.2. *(Continued)*

Prayer Number	Theme	Key Phrases and Images
35.	Educational Equality	Educational opportunity for all children, authorities and parents, fair use of public funds, sacrifice, and appreciation of good schools.
36.	Blessing of the Wanderers	Opens the hidden ways, way of the wanderer (autobiographical?), soul hungers after God, weary path without end, kinship and heritage, and peace for yearning spirits.
37.	Failure and Success	Failure and success part of life; and failures–guideposts, warnings, beacons, and guardians.
38.	Coveting	A nation of thieves; reverence for neighbor's things; thoughts, time, rights, and good name; and respect for property (institution, widow, orphan, and God).
39.	Our Global Kindred	They that sit in darkness; common humanity in love, joy, and sorrow; day when barriers fall; blood brothers in deed and word; and our greatest work.
40.	Responsibility for Failures	Failures–envy, unkindness, prejudice, hardness of heart, laziness, carelessness, repentance, and resolve.
41.	Stress and Suffering	Stress, hurt, and suffering make the person; the growing years; and respect the harder aspects of life.
42.	Worthy of One's Calling	This calling, God's goodness, and work of faith.
43.	The World of Truth	Shadows of sin; sorrow of death; and truth lies behind error, wrong, and injustice.
44.	The Old and Helpless	Unloved, uncared, and alone; responsibility for the silent sentinels of pain; and the warnings of our elders–extravagance, not dutiful and careless ease.
45.	Learning from Mistakes	Repentance, sins committed, and deeds undone; and understand the future by knowing the past.
46.	Remembering One's Home	Being true to parents' hopes, ideals, hard-earned money, love and care; and strength of home–training of children, saving of wealth, children honor parents, significance of family group, and foundations of truth and reverence.
47.	The Bonds of Poverty	Insufficient food and drink stunts growth, and feeds crime; and result of greed, selfishness, wastefulness, and willful forgetting.

Table 7.2. (Continued)

Prayer Number	Theme	Key Phrases and Images
48.	Thoughtless Acts	Persistent carelessness; deliberate evil; a mother's weary pain-scarred heart; and vision and thought.
49.	The Inner Light	Sow for the harvest; strive for that Inner Light; Joy of living; and wisdom.
50.	Love of Liberty	Cost and purpose; know the rules; Truth; and straight and narrow ways.
51.	The Importance of Schools	Training children, future work, reason and religion, heavy responsibility, and today's school is tomorrow's world.
52.	The Handicapped	Remembering the crippled and maimed, blessing of physical strength and straightness, and bodies as temples of God.
53.	Homeless and Friendless	Lay their sorrows on our hearts, atonement for our sins, goodwill toward all men, and deeds and kindness.
54.	The Value of Pride	Pride in school, race, generation, and others; racial pride; school as instrument of good; and appreciation and goodwill toward the strivings of others.
55.	Fearlessness	Confidence in the ultimate rightness of things; no fear of physical hurt, racism, or unpopularity of our cause; undismayed; fight the good fight; and face the shadow of death with courage.
56.	Thy Vision of Peace	Despise false ideals of conquest and empire; and replace force with justice and murder with relief, peace, love of country, and love of our fellow men.
57.	A Prayer for the Poor	Pity for the hungry and cold; faded memories; dedicate lives to lessening sorrow and poverty; and better life for all human souls.
58.	Love and Work	God is love; work is God's prophet; temper ambitions, and judgments; busy and sympathetic; and glory of our Life-Work.
59.	Immortality[1]	The gift of death; Easter and immortality–Christ crucified but spirit strives with men; the How, What, and Where of those many mansions; and immortality of deeds, memories, lives influenced, and ideals.

1. The prayer title was supplied by Du Bois.

Table 7.2. *(Continued)*

Prayer Number	Theme	Key Phrases and Images
60. (1)[2]	Work	Catch the thought; do the deed; create things that make life worth living; doing and striving; beauty pales; hope disappoints; and blessed is the worker.
61. (2)[2]	Christmas	Incarnate Word of God; Thy truth; Christianity is not confessions, celebrated ceremonies, and reiterated prayers; true Christianity is following the Christ spirit; and Christ spirit–poor, meek, merciful, peaceful, bow to persecution, turn the other cheek, and champion the cause of our neighbor.
62. (3)[2]	New Year	Strength, determination, and good deeds versus weakness, hesitation, and shame; prayer for courage, courtesy, goodness, strength, cheerfulness, persistence, self-control, and unselfishness; being grateful, independent, humble not slavish, reverent, and patient; faith in self; hope for our cause; and love.
63. (4)[2]	Reverence	A week of prayer; place of criticism and searching; questioning of old beliefs, ways, and deeds; recognition of error and superstition; the old and new that is good, true, and beautiful; reverent toward truth; respectful toward right; and still small voice.
64. (5)[2]	Lies	A lie is pitiable, degrading, and dangerous; honor and self-respect; great deceptions, little lies, and petty fibbing; deliverance from tattlers, tale-bearers, and liars; and lies of slavery and racial problems.
65. (6)[2]	Courtesy	Kindnesses and gentle manners, dignity and self-respect, calm quiet of conscious power, boisterousness of pretension, giving versus asking, bow unbidden, plead unanswered, and silent under scorn.
66. (7)[2]	Strength	Strength of body, mind, soul, and faith; responsibility for weakness, sickness, and death; success in study attributed to work not gift; exercise strength of character; and faith in that which is good and beautiful.
67. (8)[2]	Ambition	Aspiration and ambition, desire to be more, this mighty passion, true inspiration versus selfish temptation, healthy human being, great new century, and heritage of a mighty past.
68. (9)[2]	Persistence	Persistence in deeds and thoughts; a life worth living; snatch success and victory from failure; and never giving up.

2. Du Bois provided the prayer title and the prayer number.

Table 7.2. *(Continued)*

Prayer Number	Theme	Key Phrases and Images
69. (10)[3]	Promptness	Shame at being late; a late land and a tardy people; lingering and loafing; power found in light, movement, strength, decision, and deeds; and the tardy soul experiences neither salvation nor success.
70.	Cleanliness[1]	Cleanliness of body, thought, and soul; stealing; used postage stamps; pass bad money; keep lost articles; borrow without asking; and misuse of public property.
71.	Value of Money	Thoughtless and prodigal; the sweat, toil, and self-denial of those who love us; begging the blood of a mother's heart; useless dress and gaudy necktie; dazzle the thoughtless and weak; and time is money, money is work, work is Life, and wasting money is wasting life.

3. The number for this prayer was offered by Du Bois, but Herbert Aptheker, the editor of *Prayers for Dark People*, provided the title.

times each. Mark is cited once. The focus on Luke's gospel is not surprising given Du Bois' concern with the multitude of social issues impacting the African American community. Addressing the needs of the poor is one of the primary themes in Luke's gospel (White, 2010). Of the fifty-six prayers with scripture references, two scripture references were supplied for two of the prayers. Prayer 60, titled "Work," included an Old Testament and a New Testament reference while Prayer 65, "Courtesy," contained two New Testament references. Three Old Testament passages were cited in Prayer 66, titled "Strength."

In eight of the prayers included in *Prayers for Dark People*, Du Bois either quotes or paraphrases a verse of scripture in the main body of the prayer. The first instance of this is found in Prayer 7, which was probably intended as a recognition of Atlanta University's 1909 Commencement Day. In the latter third of the prayer, Du Bois offered a blessing, which was grounded in Numbers 6:24–26 and is then expanded. The expanded part of the blessing is in italics. The relevant text is as follows:

The Lord bless you and keep you, the Lord make his face to shine upon you and be gracious with you—the Lord lift up the Light of His countenance upon you and give you *War that out of the dust of battle and travail of soul, bitterness of defeat and anguish of sorrow, some day shall come forth the Perfect Soul.* [italics added] (Du Bois, 1980, 9)

Table 7.3. Scripture References for Prayers Included in *Prayers for Dark People*

Scripture Reference	Prayer Number	Prayer Theme/Title
Old Testament (N=37)		
Genesis 22	46	Remembering One's Home
Genesis 27:18–24	21	Honor
Genesis 32:24–32	68	Persistence
Genesis 48	44	The Old and Helpless
Exodus 12:1–3, 11–14	1	New Year's Resolution
Exodus 12:1–3, 7, 11–15	62	New Year
Leviticus 19:11–16	38	Coveting
Judges 15:11–15	66	Strength
1 Samuel 8:10–19	33	Better Government
1 Samuel 13:11–14	20	The Struggle for Freedom
1 Samuel 15	40	Responsibility for Failures
1 Samuel 16:6–12	51	The Importance of Schools
Esther 4:9–16	19	Mighty Causes
Job 6:1–4, 11–14	52	The Handicapped
Psalm 18	66	Strength
Psalm 46	24	Our Global Kin
Psalm 67	60	Work
Psalm 68:28–35	63	Reverence
Psalm 80	17	Personal Betterment
Psalm 93	66	Strength
Psalm 100	10	Thanksgiving
Psalm 119:9–16	32	Being Useful Instruments
Psalm 120	45	Learning from Mistakes
Psalm 121	55	Fearlessness
Proverbs 13:4, 7–8, 11, 18, 22–23	71	Value of Money
Ecclesiastes 2:4–11	8	Play and Recreation
Ecclesiastes 11:1–7	26	True Education
Ecclesiastes 11:6–9; 12:1–7	49	The Inner Light
Ecclesiastes 12:1–4	15	Persistence and Endurance
Isaiah 28:1–4, 7	2	The Curse of Drinking
Isaiah 43	39	Our Global Kindred
Isaiah 49:8–11	34	Success Now
Isaiah 52:1–9	67	Ambition
Joel 2:21–27	41	Stress and Suffering
Micah 4:1–4	56	Thy Vision of Peace
Micah 6:1–4,15–16	5	The Reaping of Deeds
Micah 6:1–8	27	Sins of Labor Wars
New Testament (N=23)		
Matthew 24:6–13	25	Endurance
Matthew 25:1–10	69	Promptness
Matthew 25:34–40	53	Homeless and Friendless
Matthew 25:34–40	57	A Prayer for the Poor
Mark 1:1–7	12	Advent Season
Luke 2:8–14	61	Christmas
Luke 2:40–49	35	Educational Equality
Luke 6:27–36	22	The Gift of Charity
Luke 10:30–35	65	Courtesy
Luke 15:21–28	54	The Value of Pride
Luke 16:19	47	The Bonds of Poverty
John 2:17–25	16	Persistence in Work Begun

Table 7.3. *(Continued)*

Scripture Reference	Prayer Number	Prayer Theme/Title
New Testament		
John 4:7–12	58	Love and Work
John 8:12–16	30	Truth and Ignorance
John 8:31–36	50	Love of Liberty
Acts 5:1–6	64	Lies
Acts 20:31–36	11	Joy of Giving (Advent?)
Hebrews 12:1–6	9	Summer Freedom
James 2:4–17	60	Work
James 2:14–24	14	Confidence in New Year
1 Peter 3:8–12[1]	65	Courtesy
Revelation 21:1–4[2]	4	Springtime
Revelation 22:10–17	59	Immortality
No Scripture Reference (N=15)		
	3	Peace
	6	Salvaging the Good
	7	Commencement
	13	Christmas
	18	Immortality
	23	The Gift of Death
	28	Worthy Work
	29	Simple Beauty
	31	Dedicated Students
	36	Blessing of the Wanderers
	37	Failure and Success
	42	Worthy of One's Calling
	43	The World of Truth
	48	Thoughtless Acts
	70	Cleanliness

1. Du Bois identified the scripture reference for this prayer on "Courtesy" as Peter 3:8–12. Based on the title given to the prayer, the intended reference appears to be 1 Peter 3:8–12.

2. The actual scripture reference Du Bois cites is Revelation 21:1–4, not Revelations 21:1–4. The Book of Revelation is cited correctly in the second reference (Prayer 59).

This is similar to what Biblical scholars (Perrin, 1969) describe as an editorial redaction, whereby the editor of a text will quote and/or utilize a tradition as a source and then change the text to address an issue that is of particular interest to the editor. The Numbers passage speaks of God granting peace at the very end of the blessing, but Du Bois shifts the focus to war. At this point in American society, the color line was firmly drawn, and African Americans were in the midst of a battle for self-identity and respect. Du Bois appeared to be preparing these young Atlanta University students to face the struggles and battles that lay ahead with respect to racial prejudice and inequality by charging them to work toward that day when all persons would be recognized as having equal value and worth.

Prayer 19 encouraged students to be committed to "mighty causes" like women's rights, children's education, and addressing hate, murder, and poverty. Du Bois quotes Esther 4:16b and asks students to tackle these issues with the courage of Esther as she went before the king. Du Bois quotes the first part of Jesus' beatitude concerning the meek (Matt. 5:5a) in a prayer underscoring the importance of a life characterized by charity, passion, and humility (Prayer 22). Commemorating the value of education (Prayer 26), Du Bois quotes Ecclesiastes 12:1 as a means of encouraging students to value education while they are young and education is still seen as being meaningful. Du Bois believed also that it was important for children to honor their parents. The fifth commandment on honoring one's parents (Ex. 20:12) is quoted once in Prayer 44 on the care for older persons and twice in Prayer 46 on honoring the home. Recognizing the value and importance of work in Prayer 60, Du Bois concludes the prayer by composing a beatitude honoring the worker where he maintains that the worker is blessed and the earth is the worker's kingdom. He was aware that the lack of jobs, low-wage jobs, and the exclusion of African Americans from many manufacturing jobs that paid a livable wage were primary factors impacting African American quality of life (Du Bois, 1899a/1996). The third New Year's prayer (Prayer 62) represented the last instance where Du Bois quoted scripture in the main body of one of the prayers. Desiring a year characterized by faith in each other, hope for the cause of racial equality, and love for all people, Du Bois concluded this prayer with the last verse to the Corinthian hymn to "faith, hope, and love" (1 Cor. 13:13).

Du Bois included a loose paraphrase of a stanza from Robert Browning's *Asolando* in Prayer 68 on "Persistence." Encouraging students to "never falter," he reminded them that persistence could mean the difference in one experiencing success or failure in a particular endeavor. If a leadership class was to emerge within the African American community dedicated to the task of addressing "the Negro problems," persistence would be required.

It appears that Prayers 18 and 42 were incomplete while Prayer 46 may reflect the merging of two prayers. Another prayer, Prayer 64, may have been partially edited. The two incomplete prayers address the themes of immortality (Prayer 18) and being worthy of one's calling (Prayer 42). Du Bois returns to the theme of immortality in an Easter prayer (Prayer 59). Easter is portrayed as a festival to immortality. The image of the "valley of the shadow of death" taken from Psalm 23:4 emerges again, and Du Bois' uncertainty is replaced with the assertion that people continue to live as others remember their deeds, influence, and ideals. A religious quest is experienced in the midst of uncertainty. Is this an expression of agnosticism, or could it be an example of the privatization of beliefs and represent a challenge to religious orthodoxy? Du Bois' approach to religion was complex and multilayered. The diversity of scholarly opinion as to the nature of Du Bois' beliefs and the extent of his religious involvement bears this out (Johnson, 2008; Blum, 2007; Zuckerman, 2009; Kahn, 2009).

The importance of home and parents is discussed in Prayer 46. At first glance one is tempted to treat this prayer as two prayers that have been merged. The prayer begins with the petition, "Remember with us tonight, O God, the homes that own us all." Students are then encouraged to be true to their parents by honoring their hopes, ideals, hard-earned money, and loving care. Attention shifts next to the primary functions of the home: training children and providing financial resources. This functional definition of the family echoes themes stressed in classical definitions of the family offered by Murdock (1949) and Reiss (1988). The first part of the prayer concludes with the quoting of the fifth commandment on honoring one's parents (Ex. 20:12). Next, Du Bois shifts the focus of the prayer to the home, the significance of the family as a social group, and the moral foundation supplied by homes (i.e., truth, reverence, and respect for God's Word). Du Bois closes the prayer by echoing Exodus 20:12. However, rather than merging two prayers, it actually looks like Du Bois has created a doublet, which is a commonly utilized literary device designed to provide emphasis and promote structural integration. The prayer becomes a unified whole as the main themes of each stanza alternate (home/parents to parents/home or A : B :: B : A).

The chiastic structure is another literary device employed by authors to strengthen the internal unity of a narrative. Chiastic structures are driven by a series of comparisons and contrasts. A chiastic structure may take the following form: A B C D E D' C' B' A'. A and A' represent the first pair of similar or contrasting themes. The focal point of the narrative would be "E." Focusing on the comparisons and contrasts of the main themes presented in Prayer 26 on education, the chiastic structure of the prayer is presented in the following schema.

God, give us grace (A)
    education (B)
        doing things we like (C)
        studying the tasks that appeal (C)
        wandering world of thought (C)
            universe (D)
                good–evil (E)
                pleasure–pain (E)
            learn and know (D′)
        unpleasant task (C′)
        hard lesson (C′)
        bitter experience (C′)
    knowledge, power, and good (B′)
O Lord, learn this in our youth (A′)

In this prayer one begins and ends the process of education with God's guidance. Education and knowledge are compared. Enjoyable tasks are contrasted with unpleasant ones, and the education–knowledge continuum is presented as a two-edged sword involving good and evil and pleasure and pain. The chiastic structure confirms the internal unity and consistency of the prayer.

Finally, there is some question as to whether all the "completed" prayers included in *Prayers for Dark People* are presented in their final form. The prayer on Lies (Prayer 64) is one of the longest prayers. Since the scrap of paper on which this prayer was written included two sections that had been circled, Aptheker (1980) questioned whether Du Bois intended to remove these sections. Aptheker subsequently placed the circled portions in brackets. The main body of the prayer begins with an addressing of the problems associated with lying and then pivots abruptly to a focus on the liar. On the other hand, it could be that this prayer is another example of a doublet. Du Bois begins the prayer with the phrase "Our Heavenly Father," and then, halfway through the prayer, he utilizes the phrase "Well we know, our Father." The first half of the prayer addresses lies, the middle section focuses on the liar, and the final section acknowledges slavery and racism as American society's great lies. Christians are charged to rise above society's lies. While it is possible that Du Bois could have had some second thoughts about this prayer, he did not strike through the sections that were circled, and the prayer, in its current form, preserves a progression of ideas from lies, to the liar, to society's lies.

PRAYER AS SOCIAL COMMENTARY

By 1909 Du Bois' focus was transitioning from social reform based on the presentation of empirical facts to social activism and the demand for racial equality. The prayers included in *Prayers for Dark People* document this transition, as these prayers functioned ultimately as a form of social commentary. This genre provided Du Bois with an opportunity to help children and young adults navigate experiences of double consciousness and racial inequality and to underscore the importance of their being persons of strong character, a necessary leadership quality.

Du Bois' framing of prayer as social commentary is theoretically sound. James (1902/1958) maintained that prayer is the essence of religion and is an expression of religion in action. In more recent years, Greeley (1990, 1995) has argued that religion is poetry and that the religious imagination is grounded in experiences that can be symbolized in narrative and poetic forms. Religious symbols embedded in narrative form can evoke memories of powerful experiences for hearers who share a similar cultural universe. Within this phenomenological perspective, experience provides the foundation for story, which in turn provides a basis for ritual and social structure. New Testament scholars, employing a cognitive science perspective to gain an enhanced understanding of the rise of early Christianity, maintain that texts function as symbolic scripts, which stimulate powerful thoughts, feelings, and mental images that then enable people to recall important experiences (Theissen, Chan, and Czachesz, 2017; Theissen, 2007; Czachesz, 2007, 2017). For Du Bois, it was important that the Atlanta University students understand and appreciate the African American experience and be equipped to champion social change. Prayer was a medium that allowed Du Bois to convey this message effectively.

To challenge the plausibility of existing socially constructed realities, one would need to have access to a venue that would enable one to construct a new reality. Just as the "sorrow songs" provided this venue earlier in *The Souls of Black Folk* (1903b/2007), prayers were now invoked to challenge existing realities grounded in inequality and to provide a new vision of racial equality that younger minds could embrace. So how was Du Bois able to accomplish this? Berger's (1979) concept of the "heretical imperative" provides some critical insight.

Berger maintains that the term "heresy" is rooted in the Greek word, *hairetizo*, meaning "to choose or select" (Gingrich, 1983). The heretical imperative thus addresses the religious choices that are available to persons within a society. Berger outlines three choices: the deductive option, the reductive option, and the inductive option. Persons selecting the deductive option choose to affirm religious orthodoxy and religious dogma. Existing religious worldviews are plausible. With the reductive option, the religious worldview may be replaced with a political or social worldview, and with the inductive option, persons choose to construct their own private belief system (e.g., the privatization of beliefs and the disestablishment of religion). These religious worldviews provide order in the midst of chaos as long as they remain plausible.

By the time Du Bois wrote the prayers that are now included in *Prayers for Dark People*, it was evident that, in many respects, he no longer held an orthodox Christian perspective. Berger's (1979) "deductive option" was no longer a plausible option for Du Bois. However, he still viewed the Black Church as the center of African American life and as a catalyst for social change and moral development (Du Bois, 1897b, 1899a/1996, 1900d, 1903d/2003). This perspective fits within a Progressive–Social Gospel perspective (Zuckerman, Barnes, and Cady, 2003) and would be reminiscent of Berger's "reductive option." Nevertheless, Du Bois' worldview does not fit neatly within this perspective. For Du Bois, religious symbols and imagery could be deployed to evoke images of a more perfect world that would eventually be realized on earth. Apocalyptic and eschatological language was evoked to portray a coming world that would be grounded in racial equality. The present age and the coming age were binary opposites held in dialectical tension. To prepare for this coming world, students would have to develop strong character traits like work, persistence, and a commitment to the vision. Within this "inductive" religious perspective, perhaps Du Bois was foreshadowing some of the dialectical theology of Karl Barth (1916/1968) and Rudolf Bultmann (1925/1975).

The sociology of literature perspective provides further insights into Du Bois' approach to religion, religious imagery, and religious experience. Goldmann (1966/1980, 1967/1987) argues that narratives provide portals into the social and cultural world of a text's author. To a certain extent, narratives are autobiographical. They delineate the contextual environment of those who produce them. Consequently, Du Bois' prayers functioned also as religious autobiography. The dialectical worldview could provide members of the African American community with a mechanism to navigate the realities of "double consciousness," "the veil," and "the color line," which were all brought to life in these prayers offered to Atlanta University students.

For example, Prayer 36 is dedicated to the wanderer. Perhaps Du Bois (1980, 38) was portraying himself as a wanderer whose task was to seek the "truth." During the early phase of his sociological career, Du Bois had dedicated himself to the empirical study of "the Negro problems." He believed that racial inequality was grounded in ignorance and prejudice. If inequality could be verified empirically, then social reform could be grounded in scientifically confirmed facts (Du Bois, 1898a, 1899a/1996).

Given his experiences with prejudice, discrimination, and lynchings, by 1909, Du Bois (1920, 1968/2007) realized that he could no longer address the social issues impacting the African American community from the position of a detached researcher. Advocacy was now seen as the missing link. Facts were not enough. The empirically based, scientific work of the Atlanta Sociological Laboratory and the Atlanta University Annual Conferences for the Study of the Negro Problems was being integrated with a social advocacy perspective that was reflected in Du Bois' involvement with the Niagara Movement, the founding of the NAACP, and his eventual work for the NAACP as the editor of *The Crisis*. All these activities were initiated between 1905 and 1910 as Du Bois increasingly realized that if social change was to take place, facts would have to be accompanied by actions. Perhaps Du Bois saw himself as one of these wanderers mentioned in Prayer 36 who was in search of some "Truer, Better thing—some fairer country" (Du Bois, 1908, 38). Maybe this journey was taking him from a search for empirical facts to his realization of the need to now advocate for social change more aggressively. Throughout these prayers, Du Bois was reminding the Atlanta University students of the numerous social issues impacting the African American community, but he also made them aware of their need to take responsible action if these concerns were to be addressed effectively. Persons able to accomplish this task would need to be people of strong character.

Du Bois' shift from social facts to socially informed advocacy was consistent with the Social Gospel movement, which advocated that compassion must be demonstrated rather than discussed. Walter Rauschenbusch's *Christianity and the Social Crisis* appeared in 1907. He maintained that Christianity played a key role in the social reconstruction of society. Materialism, social inequality, poverty, the plight of the worker, moral decay, the decline of the family, the misuse of power, the otherworldliness of Christianity, and the constrictive nature of religious dogma were all cited as factors limiting societal reconstruction. Summarizing the Social Gospel perspective, Rauschenbusch argued:

> It is the function of religion to teach the individual to value his soul more than his body, and his moral integrity more that his income. In the same way it is the function of religion to teach society to value human life more than property, and to value property only insofar as it forms the material basis for the higher development of human life. . . . [Religious men] should have the courage of religious faith and assert that "man liveth not by bread alone," but by doing the will of God, and that the life of a nation "consisteth not in the abundance of things" which it produces, but in the way men live justly with one another and humbly with their God. (Rauschenbusch, 1907/2007, 302)

Du Bois' insistence that the Atlanta University students develop character, a strong work ethic, a social conscience, and a willingness to practice their faith and assert it was consistent with Rauschenbusch's description of the Social Gospel and would represent a social reconstruction of society (Berger and Luckmann, 1967).

Addressing the needs of the hungry, the homeless, and the friendless (Prayers 53 and 57), Du Bois admonished students to be certain that their deeds of kindness were directed to all persons. He believed that the United States was characterized by its greed (Prayer 38) and that true faith was born of works (Prayer 14). Christianity is more than simply reciting prayers and celebrating rituals. Real Christians follow the "Christ spirit" (Prayer 13) and are willing to be poor, meek, merciful, and peaceful, suffer persecution, and champion the cause of one's neighbor (Prayer 61). Committed action trumped religious dogma, and Du Bois' understanding of what he believed to be true Christianity was consistent with the major tenets of the Social Gospel. An applied Christianity based on works could help promote social reform, social uplift, and social change. Including social and religious activism as part of his framework for addressing "the Negro problems," Du Bois (1909b/2007, 1968/2007), added the development of a social conscience and strength of character to his integrated approach to addressing and beginning to resolve key social issues impacting the African American community. Social conscience, strength of character, and applied Christianity were the cornerstones of the prayers included in *Prayers for Dark People* (1980).

So what did social conscience and strength of character include? With respect to social conscience, Du Bois wanted students to be aware of the need for a strong government that would be committed to promoting equality for all people (Prayers 3, 20, and 33). Good, quality education for all children was a necessity and a right (Prayers 26, 35, and 51). A willingness to assume responsibility for the care of older persons comes with maturity (Prayer 44), as does a heightened awareness of the needs of the poor (Prayers 19, 47, and 57), women (Prayer 19), the handicapped (Prayer 52), and the homeless (Prayer 53). An understanding of the rights of the laborer must be instilled (Prayer 27), and students were reminded that the disfranchised needed to be observant and willing to provide a critical assessment of the political process (Prayer 33). These young students were encouraged to advocate for peace rather than war and global expansion (Prayers 3 and 56) and to develop a sense of global solidarity with groups suffering injustice (Prayers 20, 24, and 39).

Character development was one of the major themes of *Morals and Manners among Negro Americans* (1914/2010), the last Atlanta University Conference report Du Bois co-directed and co-edited with Augustus Dill. This study was the sequel to *The Negro Church* (1903d/2003), and rather than being another sociological study of the Black Church as a religious organization, the focus was redirected toward an empirical investigation of African American morals and manners. The study was based on findings from a national survey that addressed such issues as good manners, sound morals, cleanliness, personal honesty, home life, the rearing of children, amusements for young people, and caring for older people. Since the majority of these topics were addressed directly in the prayers composed for the Atlanta University students between 1909 and 1910, these prayers provided an overview of some of the social issues that were impacting Du Bois at the time and perhaps were a catalyst for the 1912–1913 national survey on the state of African American character development.

In several of the prayers, the Atlanta University students were encouraged to value hard work (Prayers 28, 58, and 60), to take responsibility for their actions (Prayers 17, 40, and 45), and to learn from their successes and failures (Prayer 37). In accomplishing this, they could begin to internalize the value of nurturing such virtues as persistence and endurance (Prayers 15, 16, 25, and 68). Furthermore, model citizens would know the meaning of honor (Prayer 21), love liberty (Prayer 50), develop a healthy sense of duty (Prayer 29), be charitable (Prayers 11 and 22), value truth over ignorance (Prayer 30), practice sobriety (Prayer 2), have respect for property (Prayer 38), and honor parents (Prayer 46). Lying was unacceptable (Prayer 64), and good hygiene was to be practiced (Prayer 70). The emphasis on hygiene was one of the areas where Du Bois and Washington were in agreement (Washington, 1901/2003). However, Du Bois extended the concept of cleanliness to include body, thought, and soul. Promptness (Prayer 69), courtesy (Prayer 65), and reverence (Prayer 63) were portrayed as virtues as well.

Students were encouraged to be strong (Prayer 66), confident (Prayer 55), and driven by a healthy sense of ambition (Prayer 67). Rather than being careless and thoughtless (Prayer 48), persons should strive to be useful (Prayer 32) and to take pride in oneself so that contributions to society could be made (Prayer 54). In Prayer 54 on pride, Du Bois was able to demonstrate how one's social conscience and character complement each other. Students were reminded to be proud of their school, their identity as African Americans, and to be mindful of and recognize the quests of others. Strong homes and schools would strengthen individuals and nations, but individual success hinged on one's willingness to extend goodwill toward others. Advancement was to be attained in cooperation with others and not at the expense of others (Du Bois, 1980, 56).

Through these prayers for the Atlanta University students, Du Bois was able to provide commentary on how the world "is" as well as paint a picture of how it "should and could be." Scientific inquiry enabled Du Bois to question the plausibility of a world constructed along the color line. The next step was to take action in constructing a new social reality. *Prayers for Dark People* underscores this shift in perspective.

CHAPTER 8

The Sociological Legacy of W. E. B. Du Bois

Given the rate of knowledge expansion and expertise today, researchers trying to secure funding for research projects know that it is essential that interdisciplinary research teams be proposed and utilized. Projects often incorporate integrated, multimethod research designs. Du Bois understood the power of employing an interdisciplinary, multimethod approach to the study of "the Negro Problems" over 125 years ago. He routinely integrated historical, anthropological, sociological, and statistical approaches in his framing of these studies. This approach led to his institutionalizing methodological triangulation as a valid, reliable research perspective. Research at academic institutions today increasingly embraces applied, policy, and community-based venues, whereby scholarship and teaching can be integrated effectively (Boyer, 1996). This is seen as well in the expansion of applied and academic doctoral degree programs at universities with R1 and R2 Carnegie classifications. Du Bois' approach to the scientific, empirical nature of sociology foreshadowed this more holistic research perspective prevalent today.

Du Bois' contributions to the expansion of sociology's scientific scope, the study of urban and rural life, and the sociology of the Black Church and religion were groundbreaking and significant. The focus of his early sociological work reflected a commitment to a deliberate, intentional search for "truth." At this point in his sociological career, Du Bois believed that the systematic, scientific presentation of empirically based facts could provide a basis for social reform. Discussions of the development of sociology as a discipline within the United States and abroad that ignore Du Bois' early contributions to the field between 1897 and 1910 are incomplete.

SOCIOLOGY'S SCOPE AND METHOD

In the not too recent past, most sociology students could complete their undergraduate and graduate education without encountering Du Bois' sociological legacy. However, over the past twenty-five years, progress has been made in lifting Du Bois' sociological veil. This is evidenced in the work of Rabaka (2010), Morris (2015), Wright, II (2016a, 2016b), and Green and Wortham (2015, 2018). The recognition of the sociological legacy of this key player in the development of the American sociological tradition is long overdue.

Du Bois' study of society is grounded in the inductive method. He was a master of comparative and contextual analysis, and he believed that "the Negro Problems" were perpetuated by the continuing interplay of prejudice and ignorance. Du Bois maintained that if the scientific method was invoked in the measuring and observing of human activity, the public would be presented with a body of objective, empirical facts that could be acted upon to stimulate social reform.

Du Bois (1899a/1996) utilized methodological triangulation as a means of minimizing researcher bias. He was concerned with accurately generalizing his findings, data validity, problematic survey responses, the representative nature of samples, and problems inherent in the use of multiple interviewers. Rather than compounding errors, Du Bois believed that a multimethod research design would function as a system of checks and balances. Census findings could be confirmed, challenged, or further specified with data obtained from surveys and ethnographic analyses. Building on Booth's and Addams' early work utilizing methodological triangulation, Du Bois, early in his sociological career, institutionalized methodological triangulation as a means of minimizing researcher bias.

He understood that the study of society's focus was the investigation of human actions and not abstractions (Du Bois, 1905a/2000). Human actions could be observed and patterns of behavior that were repeatable could be identified and would provide the foundation for the formulation of data-driven "laws" of behavior. However, since humans could, to varying degrees, exercise free will, chance variations in behavior must be acknowledged. These two factors, laws and chance, framed sociology's scope as a science.

URBAN, RURAL, AND DEMOGRAPHIC STUDIES

Many of Du Bois' early sociological writings included a demographic focus. He routinely addressed such important population issues as size, composition, spatial distribution, and population dynamics. He utilized census, survey, and ethnographic data to document the social inequalities experienced by the African American community, and his commitment to this triangular methodological approach was underscored further by his insistence that sociology students at Atlanta University receive training in statistical analysis and the use of census data (Du Bois, 1903a, 1903g). Du Bois (1900c) also demonstrated how small urban and rural area studies could provide a more precise, targeted understanding of racial inequality in America.

The Philadelphia Negro, a classic study in urban sociology, was reviewed by a number of publications, including the *Journal of Political Economy* (Davis, 1900) and the *American Historical Review* (Unknown, 1900), following its initial 1899 publication. Reviewers acknowledged the thoroughness of Du Bois' analysis and recognized his objective approach to discussions of racial prejudice and discrimination. Unfortunately, this classic work in urban sociology was not reviewed in the *American Journal of Sociology*, which was founded at the University of Chicago in 1895 (Katz and Sugrue, 1998).

While Du Bois did not address population density issues directly in *The Philadelphia Negro*, he did investigate the size and the heterogeneous nature of Philadelphia's African American community. Distinct social classes within the Seventh Ward were specified, and the specific circumstances of the "submerged tenth," a group comprised of the urban poor and criminal classes, were addressed. Du Bois' identification and discussion of this group foreshadowed more recent sociological discussions of the urban underclass in the United States (Bobo, 2007; Wilson 1996, 2012). Du Bois evaluated additional structural factors impacting African American quality of life in urban settings, like organizational support networks, family structure, living conditions, and racial discrimination. However, rather than taking a "system-blame" or "culture-blame" approach to the study of social problems, Du Bois directed his efforts toward reducing structural inequality through mechanisms that promote social and economic change and social mobility.

Within this seminal study, the reader encounters early formulations of the theory of ethnic succession, the role of economic enclaves in minority communities, a functional analysis of the Black Church, and an awareness of the inverse association between mortality and social class. *The Philadelphia Negro* is a case study that demonstrates how quantitative and qualitative data analysis could be employed as complementary research approaches.

Furthermore, minority groups in urban settings and in small towns and rural communities have experienced neighborhood segregation as an outcome of prejudice and discrimination. Often this has led to specific groups being concentrated in particular geographic locations. However, within these neighborhoods, residents may begin to establish a solid economic base by developing services that meet their needs. As entrepreneurial activities become more profitable, these activities may expand to meet the needs of persons beyond the original communities of service. Portes (1987) referred to this process as the development of "economic enclaves." In discussing rural quality of life, Du Bois (1898b) suggested that similar social dynamics were operating in small rural communities like Farmville, Virginia at the end of the nineteenth century. African Americans were residing in highly segregated neighborhoods. They sponsored their own churches and social activities, and Whites were encountered primarily in the workplace. Farmville's African American community was developing business ventures that would serve their own needs, and they were becoming more selective in determining the businesses they would patronize.

This development began a process that would start to minimize Farmville's African American community's economic dependence on Whites. Consequently, a race-based system of economic dependence was gradually confronted with a more inclusive system of economic interdependence. Du Bois (1898b) believed this change would improve race relations.

While Robert Park is credited as one of the founding figures in the sociological study of race (Morris, 2007), Du Bois' Farmville study represents an early comprehensive sociological study of African American quality of life in a small rural Southern community. Rather than viewing Farmville's African American community as representing a homogeneous group, Du Bois addressed the African American experience in terms of between–racial group and within–racial group stratification. Four distinct social classes within Farmville's African American community were identified, and Du Bois expressed concern over growing class divisions within the community. This observation, along with the identification of a criminal class, foreshadowed the later work of Wilson (1996, 2009) on the internal class divisions within the African American community and the emergence of a distinct underclass.

The Farmville study was also a primer on social problems. By providing a body of scientific evidence documenting the severity of the social and economic issues faced by African Americans in small community settings like Farmville and urban settings like Philadelphia's Seventh Ward, Du Bois provided an empirical foundation, which he believed would stimulate social reform and change. The work begun with the Farmville and Philadelphia studies was continued at Atlanta University through the work of the Atlanta Sociological Laboratory and the annual Atlanta Conferences on the Study of the Negro Problems. Yet, given this massive body of social problems research, Du Bois is still rarely cited in the social problems literature. The journal *Social Problems* addressed this reality by devoting the May 2021 issue to a discussion of "The Sociology of W. E. B. Du Bois."

Although small area community studies are one of the hallmarks of the Chicago School (Calhoun, 2007), Du Bois was one of the early pioneers in this field. The Farmville study is an early example of a small area study, and in his essays addressing "the Negro problems" (Du Bois, 1898a) and the twelfth census, Du Bois (1900c) argued that census data were acceptable when trying to document broad general trends. However, small area studies would provide important details, which could not be gleaned from census data. More detailed data on topics such as occupation and wages, land and property ownership, taxation, education, crime, and voting could be provided via small area, survey-based studies. Many of these issues were addressed in Du Bois' Farmville study.

In their classic, comprehensive, empirical study of the Southern Black Belt, Wimberley and Morris (1997) argued that the region was characterized by a high rate of youth dependence, lower levels of educational attainment, and higher levels of poverty and unemployment. However, essentially one hundred years earlier, Du Bois had documented similar conditions in his study of African American quality of life in Farmville, Virginia. Limited educational opportunities, low levels of educational attainment, high levels of unemployment, and limited earnings potential as a consequence of high levels of seasonal employment were documented in the Farmville study. Furthermore, in seven additional studies, Du Bois (1899b, 1900–1902, 1901a, 1903b/2007; 1904a/1906; 1906a/2006, 1906e) continued to address issues related to the Black Belt and is thus one of the pioneering figures in the sociological study of the Southern Black Belt.

Finally, throughout his early sociological career, Du Bois made significant contributions to the development of demographic and population studies in the United States. Five of these contributions are now specified. First, he was among the first to comment on the sex ratio imbalance within the African American population (Du Bois, 1906c). Second, he documented an important migration stream from the rural South to the urban North in his discussion of the birthplace data for the African American residents of Philadelphia's Seventh Ward (Du Bois, 1899a/1996). Third, Du Bois'(1899a/1996) discussions of African American migration into slum areas and subsequently into more affluent neighborhoods anticipated the discussions of "ethnic succession" popularized later by the Chicago School (Park, Burgess, and McKenzie, 1925). Fourth, he documented important links between racial differences in mortality and variations in social class and quality of life (Du Bois, 1898b; 1899a/1996; 1906c). Fifth, the social nature of certain infectious diseases like consumption was addressed and the need for better housing, proper ventilation, exercise, and proper diet was highlighted in two book-length studies (Du Bois, 1899a/1996; 1906c).

RELIGION AND SOCIETY

In the Farmville study and in *The Philadelphia Negro*, Du Bois (1898b; 1899a/1996) offered a brief functional analysis of the Black Church and provided data on family religious identification derived from the surveys for Farmville, Virginia and Philadelphia's Seventh Ward. His studies of the Farmville and Philadelphia Black Church and the Atlanta Conference volume on *The Negro Church* (1903d/2003) represent the earliest article, book chapter, and book-length empirically based studies of a religious organization by a sociologist (Wortham, 2018b). Thus, Du Bois was a founding figure in the sociology of religion and the sociology of the Black Church.

The 1903 canvass of Atlanta's Black Churches was one of six local area social studies included in *The Negro Church*. The other local studies on the Black Church were conducted in Richmond; Chicago; Deland, Florida; Thomas County, Georgia; and Greene County, Ohio. Du Bois provided a more detailed and nuanced description of the 1903 Atlanta Black Church religious economy by collecting and analyzing ethnographic and survey data. Through the use of his trademark triangular methodology, Du Bois specified the major players in Atlanta's Black Church religious economy and identified membership patterns, involvement levels, congregational expenditures, and children's religiosity patterns. The ethnographic data provided valuable insights into the quality of pastoral leadership, the audiences attracted to certain congregations, and congregational involvement in community activities. These are the types of data that are included in contemporary congregational analysis studies (Woolever and Bruce, 2010). Furthermore, the involvement of students in the data collection process suggests that Du Bois should be included among the pioneers of the "service-learning" movement.

Applying a multidisciplinary approach to the study of the myriad social problems facing the African American community, Du Bois was able to capture the essence of quality of African American life "within the veil." Moving from the utilization of empirical facts to provide a foundation for social reform during the first years (i.e., 1897–1904) of his early sociological period, Du Bois began to assume the more active role of the informed social advocate in the later years (i.e., 1905–1910) of his early sociological period. The posthumously published *Prayers for Dark People* (1980) plays a critical role in documenting Du Bois' paradigmatic shift. Originally composed in 1909 and 1910, these prayers reinforce Du Bois' transformation from empirical sociologist to public sociologist. Thus, he may be claimed as one of the discipline's earliest public sociologists. Throughout his early sociological career, Du Bois presented his findings in technical journal articles and in the popular press. The prayer venue provided one more example of how Du Bois was able to use a variety of avenues to communicate and share the quality of life challenges faced by the African American community with a larger, more diverse audience.

Recognizing the importance of the Black Church in the life of African Americans, particularly in the South, Du Bois understood that prayer, like the sorrow songs in *The Souls of Black Folk* (1903), could be utilized as an effective medium of identity formation, socialization, and enculturation. The prayer format was a particularly effective tool for reaching a much younger audience. More specifically, these prayers represented Du Bois' first formal attempt to introduce African American children and young adults to the scope and significance of "the Negro problems."

On one level, the prayers included in *Prayers for Dark People* provided social commentary on the everyday life experiences of persons within the African American community. They were utilized also to raise social consciousness and to invoke a call to action. Professing one's religious faith was not enough. Real Christianity was revealed in actions and deeds. Du Bois (1980) encouraged his young hearers to take their studies seriously and to empathize with the needs and concerns of others. Students were invited to be part of the construction of a new social reality based on the principle of racial equality. However, to join this venture, one must also be willing to assume responsibility for one's actions, be persons of good character and sound morals, and think of others as well as oneself. Through these prayers Du Bois was able to provide commentary on how the world "is" as well as paint a picture of how it "could and should be."

CONCLUSION

Du Bois' shift from empirical sociologist to public sociologist is documented through the following three examples. First, even though Du Bois had collaborated with Booker T. Washington in providing essays that were included in the 1907 volume *The Negro in the South*, by 1909, the Washington–Du Bois conflict was reaching a climax. Du Bois (1968/2007) believed that the "Tuskegee Machine" had unfavorably impacted his ability to secure funds to support the activities of the annual Atlanta University Conferences, and he was satisfied no longer with just being able to present empirical facts related to a social issue.

Second, also by 1909, Du Bois was aware that the U.S. Department of Labor would not publish his massive 1906 Lowndes County, Alabama social study because it dealt with controversial issues like African American disfranchisement and land ownership (Du Bois, 1909a, 1968/2007; Grossman, 1974; D. Lewis, 2009). Reflecting on this study later in life, Du Bois (1968/2007) believed that the Lowndes County study represented some of his best sociological work. Some of the social issues that were to be addressed in this unpublished empirical study appear to have resurfaced in Du Bois' first novel, *The Quest for the Silver Fleece* (1911c/2007), which in many respects was an example of historical fiction. This work addressed educational inequalities and the economic challenges faced by African American farm laborers and landowners. The silver fleece was a symbol for cotton, which served as currency in the agricultural economy. An Alabama county was also one of the settings for the novel.

Third, the 1906 Atlanta riots and the lynching of African Americans made it impossible for Du Bois to remain a detached academician. Consequently, at this point in his career, Du Bois began to shift his emphasis toward an organized quest for racial justice through the work of the Niagara movement and the NAACP. The emphasis on "what is" was now being replaced with a focus on "what ought to be" as the gap between ideal culture and real culture widened within Du Bois' evolving new perspective. In this context Du Bois' focus on character in the prayers to the Atlanta University students was aimed to strengthen and motivate them as they matured and prepared for the continuing struggle for racial equality. Also in 1909, Du Bois published his first book-length biography, *John Brown*. Rather than providing a traditional historical account of the abolitionist's life, Du Bois showcased Brown as a role model in the fight for social justice.

Du Bois left Atlanta University in 1910 to assume the editorship of the NAACP's *The Crisis*. However, while at Atlanta University, he established a sociological legacy. Students received sound sociological training. A research center was maintained (i.e., the Atlanta Sociological Laboratory) with Du Bois as a key figure; research findings were published through the Atlanta University Conference annual reports; funding was sought by the center from such funding sources as the Carnegie Institution and the John F. Slater Fund, and members of the Atlanta community and the larger research community were invited to participate in the center's activities (Wright, 2002a, 2002b, 2006, 2008, 2016; Wright and Calhoun 2006). Methodological triangulation was a recognizable, trademark research design for the studies conducted by the Atlanta Sociological Laboratory, and historical and ethnographic findings were consistently coupled with census and survey findings to provide a more comprehensive portrayal of African American quality of life. All of these activities were accomplished by Du Bois and Atlanta University between 1897 and 1910 while the early work on community studies by the "Chicago School" was being conducted as well. Thus, the volume of Du Bois' early sociological work bears testimony to his role as a pioneering figure in the development of empirical and public sociology in the United States and globally. W. E. B. Du Bois was a pioneer American sociologist and a world-renowned classical sociologist.

Appendix

A Du Bois Primer

This primer is a quick guide to some of W. E. B. Du Bois' key sociological ideas and writings. Included are a list of key concepts, several classic quotes from Du Bois' early sociological writings, and a list of selected core books and articles. To assist those who want to take a deeper dive into Du Bois' works, two websites are provided. These sites provide access to digital versions of many primary sources. A brief selection of key secondary sources on Du Bois' early sociological period at Atlanta University and his work with the Atlanta Sociological Laboratory and the annual Atlanta University Conferences on the Study of the Negro Problems provides readers and researchers with additional insight into Du Bois' early, pioneering sociological work.

KEY CONCEPTS

The Negro problems
The legacy of slavery
Quest for the truth (empirical truth versus ignorance)
The color line
Double consciousness
The veil
Empirical sociology ("what is" versus "what ought to be")
Methodological triangulation
Sociology is a science (laws and chance)
The talented tenth
The 100-year program (annual Atlanta University Conferences)

Atlanta Sociological Laboratory
Social uplift (social mobility)
African culture and civilization
Art and propaganda
Souls of Black folk and White folk

CLASSIC QUOTES

"It is a peculiar sensation, this double consciousness, this sense of always looking at one's self through the eyes of others." (Strivings of the Negro People, 1897)

"The utmost that the world can demand is not lack of human interest and moral conviction, but rather the heart quality of fairness, and an earnest desire for the truth despite its possible unpleasantness." (*The Philadelphia Negro*, 1899)

"The problem of the twentieth century is the problem of the color line; the relation of the darker to the lighter races of men in Asia and Africa, in America and the islands of the sea." (The Freedman's Bureau, 1901)

"Chance—that is actions undetermined by and independent of actions gone before. The duty of science, then, is the Science that seeks the limits of Chance in human conduct. . . . Sociology, then, is the Science that seeks the limits of Chance in human conduct." (Sociology Hesitant, 1905)

"He who would tell a tale must look toward three ideals: to tell it well, to tell it beautifully, and to tell the truth." (*The Quest of the Silver Fleece*, 1911)

"My real life work was done at Atlanta for thirteen years, from my twenty-ninth to my forty-second birthday. They were years of great spiritual upturning, of the making and unmaking of ideals, hard work and hard play. Here I found myself. I lost most of my mannerisms. I grew more broadly human, made my closest and most holy friendships, and studied human beings." (*Darkwater*, 1920)

"One could not be a calm, cool, and detached scientist while Negroes were lynched, murdered and starved." (*The Autobiography of W. E. B. Du Bois*, 1968)

CORE DU BOIS BOOKS

The Suppression of the African Slave-Trade to the United States of America, 1638–1870 (1896)
The Philadelphia Negro: A Social Study (1899)
The Souls of Black Folk (1903)
John Brown (1909)
The Quest of the Silver Fleece (1900)
Darkwater: Voices from within the Veil (1920)
The Gift of Black Folk: The Negroes in the Making of America (1924)
Black Reconstruction (1935)
Dusk of Dawn: An Essay toward an Autobiography of a Race Concept (1940)
The Autobiography of W. E. B. Du Bois: A Soliloquy on Viewing My Life from the Last Decade of Its First Century (1968)

These books are part of the Oxford W. E. B. Du Bois series, edited by Henry Louis Gates, Jr., and published by Oxford University Press in 2007.

CORE DU BOIS ARTICLES

A program for a sociological society. (1897). W. E. B. Du Bois Papers (MS 312). Special Collections and University Archives, University of Massachusetts Amherst Libraries.
The conservation of races. (1897) American Negro Academy, Occasional Papers No. 2. Washington, DC: American Negro Academy.
The problem of amusement. *The Southern Workman*, 27 (1897), 184.
The study of the Negro problems. *Annals of the American Academy of Political and Social Science*, 11 (1898), 1–23.
The Negroes of Farmville, Virginia. *Bulletin of the Department of Labor* 14 (1898), 1–38.
The Atlanta University conferences. *Charities*, 10 (1903), 435–439.
The laboratory in sociology at Atlanta University. *Annals of the American Academy of Political and Social Science*, 21 (1903), 503–505.

The talented tenth (1903). In B. Washington, W. Du Bois, P. Dunbar, C. Chestnutt, and others, *The Negro Problem: A Series of Articles by Representative American Negroes of To-day* (33–75). New York: James Pott.

Sociology hesitant. (1905). Previously unpublished article originally published in *Boundary* 2, 27 (2000), 37–44.

Die Negerfrage in den Vereinigten Staaten. *Archiv fur Sozialwissenschaft und Sozialpolitik*, 22 (1906), 241–290. Translated by J. Fracchia and published 100 years later as The Negro question in the United States. *New Centennial Review*, 6 (2006), 241–290.

Race friction between Blacks and Whites. *American Journal of Sociology*, 12 (1908), 834–838.

The souls of White folk. *Independent*, 69 (1910), 339–342.

SELECTED SECONDARY SOURCES ON DU BOIS' EARLY SOCIOLOGICAL PERIOD

Battle-Baptist, W.; & Russert, B. (Eds.). (2018). *W. E. B. Du Bois's data portraits visualizing Black America: the color line at the turn of the twentieth century*. New York: Princeton Architectural Press.

Lewis, D. L. (2009). *W. E. B. Du Bois: a biography, 1868–1963*. New York: Henry Holt.

Morris, A. (2015). *The scholar denied: W. E. B. Du Bois and the birth of modern sociology*. Oakland: University of California Press.

Rabaka, R. (2010). *Against epistemic apartheid: W. E. B. Du Bois and the Disciplinary Decadence of Sociology*. Lanham, MD: Lexington Books.

Wortham, R. (Ed.). (2009). *W. E. B. Du Bois and the sociological imagination: a reader, 1897–1914*. Waco, TX: Baylor University Press.

Wortham, R. (Ed.). (2011). *The Sociological Souls of Black Folk: Essays by W. E. B. Du Bois*. Introduction, Reconstructed Essay, and Additional Editing by R. Wortham. Lanham, MD: Lexington Books (paperback 2013).

Wright, E. II. (2016). *W. E. B. Du Bois and the Atlanta sociological laboratory: the first American school of sociology*. Farnham, UK: Ashgate.

KEY WEB SITES

http://webdubois.org
http://credo.library.umass/

References

Addams, J. (1895). *Hull-House maps and papers*. New York: Thomas Y. Crowell.

Ammerman, N.; Carroll, J.; Dudley, C.; & McKinney, W. (1998). *Studying congregations: a new handbook*. Nashville: Abingdon Press.

Anderson, E. (1996). Introduction. In W. E. B. Du Bois, *The Philadelphia Negro: a social study* (ix–xxxvi). Philadelphia: University of Pennsylvania Press.

Aptheker, H. (1997). *The correspondence of W. E. B. Du Bois: volume I selections, 1877–1934*. Amherst: University of Massachusetts Press.

Aptheker, H. (1980). Introduction. In W. E. B. Du Bois, *Prayers for dark people*, H. Aptheker, Ed. (v–xi). Amherst: University of Massachusetts Press.

Babbie, E. (2016). *The basics of social research* (7th ed.). Belmont, CA: Cengage Learning.

Baer, H.; & Singer, M. (1992). *African-American religion in the twentieth century: varieties of protest and accommodation*. Knoxville: University of Tennessee Press.

Barth, K. (1916/1968). *The epistle to the Romans*. New York: Oxford University Press.

Battle-Baptiste, W.; & Russert, B. (Eds.). (2018). *W. E. B. Du Bois's data portraits visualizing Black America: the color line at the turn of the twentieth century*. New York: Princeton Architectural Press.

Berger, P. (1963). *Invitation to sociology: a humanistic perspective*. New York: Doubleday.

Berger, P. (1979). *The heretical imperative*. Garden City, NY: Anchor Press/Doubleday.

Berger, P.; & Luckmann, T. (1967). *The social construction of reality: a treatise in the sociology of knowledge*. New York: Anchor Books.

Billingsley, A. (1999). *Mighty like a river: the Black church and social reform*. New York: Oxford University Press.

Blum, E. (2007). *W. E. B. Du Bois: American prophet*. Philadelphia: University of Pennsylvania Press.

Bobo, L. (2007). Introduction. In W. E. B. Du Bois, *The Philadelphia Negro: a social study* (xxv–xxx). New York: Oxford University Press.

Bonacich, E. (1972). A theory of ethnic antagonism: the split labor market. *American Sociological Review, 37*, 547–559.

Bonacich, E. (1976). Advanced capitalism and Black/White race relations in the United States: a split labor market interpretation. *American Sociological Review, 41*, 34–51.

Booth, C. (1892–1897). *Life and labour of the people in London*. (Vols. 1–9 plus maps.) London: Macmillan.

Boston, T. (1991). W. E. B. Du Bois and the historical school of economics. *American Economic Review*, 81, 303–306.

Boyer, E. (1996). From scholarship reconsidered to scholarship assessed. *Quest*, 48, 129–139.

Broderick, F. 1958. The academic training of W. E. B. DuBois. *Journal of Negro Education*, 27, 10–16.

Bultmann, R. (1925/1975). Das problem einer theologischen exegese des neuen testaments. In G. Strecker (Ed.), *Das Problem der Theologie des Neuen Testaments* (249–277). Darmstadt: Wissenschaftliche Buchgesellschaft.

Calhoun, C. (2007). Sociology in America: an introduction. In C. Calhoun (Ed.), *Sociology in America: a history* (1–38). Chicago: University of Chicago Press.

Cooper, A. (1892). *A voice from the South*. Xenia, OH: Aldine Printing House.

Czachesz, I. (2007). The transmission of early Christian thought: toward a cognitive psychological model. *Studies in Religion/Sciences Religieuses*, 36, 65–84.

Czachesz, I. (2017). *Cognitive science and the New Testament: a new approach to early Christian research*. New York: Oxford University Press.

Davis, K. (1900). The condition of the Negro in Philadelphia. *Journal of Political Economy*, 8, 248–260.

Du Bois, W. E. B. (1897a). A program for a sociological society, 1897. Unpublished speech in W. E. B. Du Bois Papers (MS 312). Special Collections and University Archives, University of Massachusetts Amherst Libraries.

Du Bois, W. E. B. (1897b). The problem of amusement. *Southern Workman*, 27, 181–184.

Du Bois, W. E. B. (1898a). The study of the Negro problems. *Annals of the American Academy of Political and Social Science*, 11, 1–23.

Du Bois, W. E. B. (1898b). The Negroes of Farmville, Virginia: a social study. United States Department of Labor. *Bulletin* 3, no. 14, 1–38.

Du Bois, W. E. B. (1899a/1996). *The Philadelphia Negro: a social study*, introduction by E. Anderson. Philadelphia: University of Pennsylvania Press.

Du Bois, W. E. B. (1899b). The Negro in the Black Belt: some social sketches." United States Department of Labor. *Bulletin* 4, no. 22, 401–417.

Du Bois, W. E. B. (1899c). *Some efforts of American Negroes for their own social betterment*. Atlanta: Atlanta University Press.

Du Bois, W. E. B. (1900a). The Georgia Negro: a social study. Paris Exposition (*Exposition Universelle*), April 15–November 12, 1900. The Negro Exhibit. http://129.171.53.1/ep/Paris/home.htm and http://hdl.loc.gov/loc.pnp/ppmsca.33863. Reprinted in 2018 as *W. E. B. Du Bois's data portraits visualizing Black America: the color line at the turn of the twentieth century*, W. Battle-Baptiste and B. Russert (Eds.). New York: Princeton Architectural Press.

Du Bois, W. E. B. (1900b). Post graduate work in sociology in Atlanta University, 1900. Unpublished speech in W. E. B. Du Bois Papers (MS 312). Special Collections and University Archives, University of Massachusetts Amherst Libraries.

Du Bois, W. E. B. (1900c). The twelfth census and the Negro problems. *Southern Workman*, 29, 305–309.

Du Bois, W. E. B. (1900d). The religion of the American Negro. *New World*, 9, 614–625.

Du Bois, W. E. B. (1900–1902). Testimony of Prof. W. E. Burghardt Du Bois. In *Report of the industrial commission on education* (159–175). Washington, DC.: United States Industrial Commission Reports, Volume 15.

Du Bois, W. E. B. (1901a). The Negro landholder of Georgia. United States Department of Labor. *Bulletin* 6, no. 35, 647–777.

Du Bois, W. E. B. (1901b). The Black north: a social study. The series of five articles was published by *The New York Times* between November and December 1901. Reprinted in 1969 as *The Black north: a social study.* New York: Arno Press.

Du Bois, W. E. B. (1902a). Letter from United States Bureau of Labor to W. E. B. Du Bois, July 28, 1902. W. E. B. Du Bois Papers (MS 312), Special Collections and University Archives, University of Massachusetts Amherst Libraries.

Du Bois, W. E. B. (1902b). *The Negro artisan.* Atlanta: Atlanta University Press.

Du Bois, W. E. B. (1903a). The Atlanta University conferences. *Charities,* 10, 435–439.

Du Bois, W. E. B. (1903b/2007). *The souls of Black folk.* H. L. Gates, Jr. (Ed.) and introduction by A. Rampersad. New York: Oxford University Press.

Du Bois, W. E. B. (1903c). The talented tenth. In *The Negro problem: a series of articles by representative American Negroes of to-day* (33–75). Contributions by Booker T. Washington, W. E. Burghardt Du Bois, Paul Laurence Dunbar, Charles W. Chestnutt, and others. New York: James Pott.

Du Bois, W. E. B. (1903d/2003). *The Negro church.* Introduction by P. Zuckerman, S. Barnes & D. Cady. Walnut Creek, CA: AltaMira Press.

Du Bois, W. E. B. (1903e). Letter from United States Census Office to W. E. B. Du Bois, February 21, 1903. W. E. B. Du Bois Papers (MS 312), Special Collections and University Archives, University of Massachusetts Amherst Libraries.

Du Bois, W. E. B. (1903f). Letter from W. E. B. Du Bois to the United States Census Office, No date. W. E. B. Du Bois Papers (MS 312), Special Collections and University Archives, University of Massachusetts Amherst Libraries.

Du Bois, W. E. B. (1903g). The laboratory in sociology at Atlanta University. *Annals of the American Academy of Political and Social Science,* 21, 503–505.

Du Bois, W. E. B. (1904a). The Negro farmer. United States Department of Labor. *Bulletin* 8, 69–98. Supplemental material provided in 1906 in United States Department of Commerce and Labor, Bureau of the Census. (1906). *Special reports: supplementary analysis and derivative tables. Twelfth census of the United States, 1900,* Part 2 (511–579). Washington, DC: Government Printing Office.

Du Bois, W. E. B. (1904b). The development of a people. *International Journal of Ethics,* 14, 292–311.

Du Bois, W. E. B. (1904c). Credo. *The Independent,* 57, 787.

Du Bois, W. E. B. (1904d). *Some notes on Negro crime particularly in Georgia.* Atlanta: Atlanta University Press.

Du Bois, W. E. B. (1904e). Letter from United States Bureau of Labor to W. E. B. Du Bois, April 18, 1904. W. E. B. Du Bois Papers (MS 312), Special Collections and University Archives, University of Massachusetts Amherst Libraries.

Du Bois, W. E. B. (1904f). The Atlanta conferences. *Voice of the Negro,* 1, 85–89.

Du Bois, W. E. B. (1905a/2000). Sociology hesitant. *Boundary 2,* 27, 37–44.

Du Bois, W. E. B. (1905b). Atlanta University. In R. Ogden (Ed.), *From servitude to service: being the old South lectures on the history and work of Southern institutions for the education of the Negro* (155–197). Boston: American Unitarian Association.

Du Bois, W. E. B. (1905c). A proposed study of a Black Belt county, 1905, No date. W. E. B. Du Bois Papers (MS 312), Special Collections and University Archives, University of Massachusetts Amherst Libraries.

Du Bois, W. E. B. (1905d). A proposed study of a Black Belt county, 1905 (typed version), no date. W. E. B. Du Bois Papers (MS 312), Special Collections and University Archives, University of Massachusetts Amherst Libraries.

Du Bois, W. E. B. (1905e). Industrial conditions of the Black Cotton Belt, 1905, no date. W. E. B. Du Bois Papers (MS 312), Special Collections and University Archives, University of Massachusetts Amherst Libraries.

Du Bois, W. E. B. (1905f). Notes for Lowndes County study [fragment], 1905, no date. W. E. B. Du Bois Papers (MS 312), Special Collections and University Archives, University of Massachusetts Amherst Libraries.

Du Bois, W. E. B. (1905g). Memoranda, 1905, no date. W. E. B. Du Bois Papers (MS 312), Special Collections and University Archives, University of Massachusetts Amherst Libraries.

Du Bois, W. E. B. (1906a). Die Negerfrage in den Vereinigten Staaten. *Sozialpolitik*, 22, 21–79. Reprinted and translated by J. Fracchia as The Negro question in the United States. *New Centennial Review*, 6, 2006, 241–290.

Du Bois, W. E. B. (1906b). A litany at Atlanta. *The Independent*, 61, 856–858.

Du Bois, W. E. B. (1906c). *The health and physique of the Negro American*. Atlanta: Atlanta University Press.

Du Bois, W. E. B. (1906d). The economic future of the Negro. *Publications of the American Economic Association*, 7, 219–242.

Du Bois, W. E. B. (1906e). Schedule for Lowndes County, Alabama, 1906. W. E. B. Du Bois Papers (MS 312), Special Collections and University Archives, University of Massachusetts Amherst Libraries.

Du Bois, W. E. B. (1906f). Letter from W. E. B. Du Bois to United States Bureau of Labor, January 19, 1906. W. E. B. Du Bois Papers (MS 312), Special Collections and University Archives, University of Massachusetts Amherst Libraries.

Du Bois, W. E. B. (1906g). Letter from John Lemon to W. E. B. Du Bois, January 23, 1906. W. E. B. Du Bois Papers (MS 312), Special Collections and University Archives, University of Massachusetts Amherst Libraries.

Du Bois, W. E. B. (1906h). Letter from John Lemon to W. E. B. Du Bois, June 22, 1906. W. E. B. Du Bois Papers (MS 312), Special Collections and University Archives, University of Massachusetts Amherst Libraries.

Du Bois, W. E. B. (1906i). Letter from W. E. B. Du Bois to United States Bureau of Labor, July 9, 1906. W. E. B. Du Bois Papers (MS 312), Special Collections and University Archives, University of Massachusetts Amherst Libraries.

Du Bois, W. E. B. (1906j). Letter from United States Bureau of Labor to W. E. B. Du Bois, July 24, 1906. W. E. B. Du Bois Papers (MS 312), Special Collections and University Archives, University of Massachusetts Amherst Libraries.

Du Bois, W. E. B. (1906k). Notes for Lowndes County study by unknown author. List of data that need to be collected, no date. W. E. B. Du Bois Papers (MS 312), Special Collections and University Archives, University of Massachusetts Amherst Libraries.

Du Bois, W. E. B. (1907a). Religion in the south. In B. Washington and W. E. B. Du Bois, *The Negro in the south* (125–91, 214–22). Philadelphia: George W. Jacobs.

Du Bois, W. E. B. (1907b). *Economic co-operation among Negro Americans*. Atlanta: Atlanta University Press.

Du Bois, W. E. B. (1907c). Memorandum from W. E. B. Du Bois to United States Bureau of Labor, February 16, 1907. W. E. B. Du Bois Papers (MS 312), Special Collections and University Archives, University of Massachusetts Amherst Libraries.

Du Bois, W. E. B. (1907d). Letter from United States Bureau of Labor to W. E. B. Du Bois, February 28, 1907. W. E. B. Du Bois Papers (MS 312), Special Collections and University Archives, University of Massachusetts Amherst Libraries.

Du Bois, W. E. B. (1907e). Letter from W. E. B. Du Bois to United States Bureau of Labor, March 6, 1907. W. E. B. Du Bois Papers (MS 312), Special Collections and University Archives, University of Massachusetts Amherst Libraries.

Du Bois, W. E. B. (1907f). Letter from United States Bureau of Labor to W. E. B. Du Bois, March 19, 1907. W. E. B. Du Bois Papers (MS 312), Special Collections and University Archives, University of Massachusetts Amherst Libraries.

Du Bois, W. E. B. (1907g). Letter from United States Bureau of Labor to W. E. B. Du Bois, March 27, 1907. W. E. B. Du Bois Papers (MS 312), Special Collections and University Archives, University of Massachusetts Amherst Libraries.

Du Bois, W. E. B. (1907h). Letter from United States Bureau of Labor to W. E. B. Du Bois, May 10, 1907. W. E. B. Du Bois Papers (MS 312), Special Collections and University Archives, University of Massachusetts Amherst Libraries.

Du Bois, W. E. B. (1907i). Letter from United States Bureau of Labor to W. E. B. Du Bois, August 30, 1907. W. E. B. Du Bois Papers (MS 312), Special Collections and University Archives, University of Massachusetts Amherst Libraries.

Du Bois, W. E. B. (1907j). Letter from W. E. B. Du Bois to United States Bureau of Labor, October 8, 1907. W. E. B. Du Bois Papers (MS 312), Special Collections and University Archives, University of Massachusetts Amherst Libraries.

Du Bois, W. E. B. (1907k). Letter from United States Bureau of Labor to W. E. B. Du Bois, November 2, 1907. W. E. B. Du Bois Papers (MS 312), Special Collections and University Archives, University of Massachusetts Amherst Libraries.

Du Bois, W. E. B. (1908a). *The Negro American family*. Atlanta: Atlanta University Press.

Du Bois, W. E. B. (1908b). Letter from United States Department of Commerce to W. E. B. Du Bois, June 3, 1908. W. E. B. Du Bois Papers (MS 312), Special Collections and University Archives, University of Massachusetts Amherst Libraries.

Du Bois, W. E. B. (1908c). Letter from United States Treasury Department to W. E. B. Du Bois, June 12, 1908. W. E. B. Du Bois Papers (MS 312), Special Collections and University Archives, University of Massachusetts Amherst Libraries.

Du Bois, W. E. B. (1908d). Letter from United States Bureau of Labor to W. E. B. Du Bois, November 9, 1908. W. E. B. Du Bois Papers (MS 312), Special Collections and University Archives, University of Massachusetts Amherst Libraries.

Du Bois, W. E. B. (1908e). Letter from W. E. B. Du Bois to United States Bureau of Labor, February 6, 1908. W. E. B. Du Bois Papers (MS 312), Special Collections and University Archives, University of Massachusetts Amherst Libraries.

Du Bois, W. E. B. (1908f). Letter from W. E. B. Du Bois to John W. Lemon, May 1, 1908. W. E. B. Du Bois Papers (MS 312), Special Collections and University Archives, University of Massachusetts Amherst Libraries.

Du Bois, W. E. B. (1908g). Letter from Monroe Work to W. E. B. Du Bois, October 1, 1908. W. E. B. Du Bois Papers (MS 312), Special Collections and University Archives, University of Massachusetts Amherst Libraries.

Du Bois, W. E. B. (1908h). Letter from W. E. B. Du Bois to United States Bureau of Labor, November 7, 1908. W. E. B. Du Bois Papers (MS 312), Special Collections and University Archives, University of Massachusetts Amherst Libraries.

Du Bois, W. E. B. (1909a). Letter from W. E. B. Du Bois to Henry W. Farnam, April 22, 1909. W. E. B. Du Bois Papers (MS 312), Special Collections and University Archives, University of Massachusetts Amherst Libraries.

Du Bois, W. E. B. (1909b/2007). *John Brown*. H. L. Gates, Jr. (Ed.), and introduction by P. Finkelman. New York: Oxford University Press.

Du Bois, W. E. B. (1910). The souls of White folk. *The Independent*, 61, 339–342.

Du Bois, W. E. B. (1911a). The economics of Negro emancipation in the United States. *Sociological Review*, 4, 303–313.

Du Bois, W. E. B. (1911b). The evolution of the Black south. *American Negro Monographs*, 1, 3–12.

Du Bois, W. E. B. (1911c/2007). *The quest of the silver fleece*. H. L. Gates, Jr. (Ed.), and introduction by W. Andrews. New York: Oxford University Press.

Du Bois, W. E. B. (1912). The rural south. *American Statistical Association Publications*, 13, no. 97, 80–84.

Du Bois, W. E. B. (1913). The social effects of Emancipation. *Survey*, 29, 570–573.

Du Bois, W. E. B. (1920). *Darkwater: voices from within the veil*. New York: Harcourt, Brace and Howe.

Du Bois, W. E. B. (1935/2007). *Black reconstruction in America*. H. L. Gates, Jr. (Ed.), and introduction by D. L. Lewis. New York: Oxford University Press.

Du Bois, W. E. B. (1940/2007). *Dusk of dawn: an essay towards an autobiography of a race concept*. H. L. Gates, Jr. (Ed.), and introduction by K. A. Appiah. New York: Oxford University Press.

Du Bois, W. E. B. (1968/2007). *The autobiography of W. E. B. Du Bois: a soliloquy on viewing my life from the last decade of its first century*. H. L. Gates, Jr. (Ed.), and introduction by W. Sollors. New York: Oxford University Press.

Du Bois, W. E. B. (1980). *Prayers for dark people*. H. Aptheker. (Ed.). Amherst: University of Massachusetts Press.

Du Bois, W. E. B.; & Dill, A. (1912). *The Negro American artisan*. Atlanta: Atlanta University Press.

Du Bois, W. E. B.; & Dill, A. (1914/2010). *Morals and manners among Negro Americans*. R. Wortham (Ed.). Lanham, MD: Lexington Books.

Durkheim, E. (1897/1966). *Suicide: a study in sociology*. J. Spaulding and G. Simpson (Trans.), and G. Simpson (Ed.). New York: Free Press.

Durkheim, E. (1912/1995). *The elementary forms of religious life*. K. Fields (Trans.). New York: Free Press.

Ellison, C.; & Sherkat, D. (1995). The semi-involuntary institution revisited: regional variations in church participation among Black Americans. *Social Forces*, 73, 1415–1437.

Finke, R.; & Stark, R. (2000). *Acts of faith: explaining the human side of religion*. Berkeley: University of California Press.

Finke, R.; & Stark, R. (2005). *The churching of America, 1776–2005* (2nd ed.). New Brunswick, NJ: Rutgers University Press.

Fischer, W. (1968). Gustav Schmoller. In D. Sills (Ed.), *International Encyclopedia of the Social Sciences*, Vol. 14 (60–63). New York: Macmillan and Free Press.

Fluker, W. (2016). *The ground has shifted: the future of the Black church in post-racial America*. New York: New York University Press.

Fowler, J. (1981). *Stages of faith: the psychology of human development and the quest for meaning*. San Francisco: Harper & Row.

Frazier, E. (1964). *The Negro church in America*. New York: Schocken.

Gates, H. L., Jr. (2021). *The Black church: this is our story, this is our song*. New York: Penguin Press.

Giddings, F. (1896). *The principles of sociology: an analysis of the phenomena of association and of social organization*. New York: Macmillan.

Gingrich, F. (1983). *Shorter lexicon of the Greek New Testament* (2nd ed.). Revised by F. Danker. Chicago: University of Chicago Press.

Goldmann, L. (1966/1980). *Essays on method in the sociology of literature*. W. Boelhower, (Ed.). New York: Telos Press.

Goldmann, L. (1967/1987). *Towards a sociology of the novel*. London: Tavistock.

Grammich, J.; Hadaway, K.; Housel, R.; Jones, D.; Krindatch, A.; Stanley, R.; & Taylor, R. (2012). *2010 U.S. religion census: religious congregations & membership study*. Conducted by the Association of Statisticians of American Religious Bodies (ASARB). Lenexa, KS: Foundry Publishing.

Greeley, A. (1990). *The Catholic myth: the behavior and beliefs of American Catholics*. New York: Collier.

Greeley, A. (1995). *Religion as poetry*. New Brunswick, NJ: Transaction Publishers.

Green, D.; & Wortham, R. (2015). Sociology hesitant: the continuing neglect of W. E. B. Du Bois. *Sociological Spectrum*, 35, 518–533.

Green, D.; & Wortham, R. (2018). The sociological insight of W. E. B. Du Bois. *Sociological Inquiry*, 88, 56–78.

Grossman, J. (1974). Black studies in the department of labor, 1897–1907. *Monthly Labor Review*, 97, 17–27.

Guttentag, M.; & Secord, P. (1983). *Too many women? the sex ratio question*. Beverly Hills, CA: Sage.

Hadaway, C.; Marler, P. & Chaves, M. (1993). What the polls don't show: a closer look at U.S. church attendance. *American Sociological Review*, 58, 741–752.

James, W. (1902/1958). *The varieties of religious experience*. Foreword by J. Barzun. New York: New American Library.

Jelen, T. (2002). *Sacred markets, sacred canopies: essays on religious markets and religious pluralism*. Lanham, MD: Rowman & Littlefield.

Johnson, B. (2008). *W. E. B. Du Bois: toward agnosticism, 1868–1934*. Lanham, MD: Rowman & Littlefield.

Johnstone, R. (2016). *Religion in society: a sociology of religion* (8th ed.). New York: Routledge.

Kahn, J. (2009). *Divine discontent: the religious imaginations of W. E. B. Du Bois*. New York: Oxford University Press.

Katz, M.; & Sugrue, T. (1998). The context of *The Philadelphia Negro*: the city, the Settlement House Movement, and the rise of the social sciences. In M. Katz & T. Sugrue (Eds.), *W. E. B. DuBois, race, and the city:* The Philadelphia Negro *and its legacy* (1–37). Philadelphia: University of Pennsylvania Press.

Kosmin, B.; & Keysar, A. 2006. *Religion in a free market: religious and non-religious Americans, who/what/why/where.* Ithaca, NY: Paramount Market.

Lewis, D. (2009). *W. E. B. Du Bois: a biography, 1868–1963.* New York: Henry Holt.

Lewis, O. (1966). The culture of poverty. *Scientific* American, 215, 19–25.

Lincoln, C.; & Mamiya, L. (1990). *The Black church in the African American experience.* Durham, NC: Duke University Press.

Lowndes County, Alabama. Population 2022. https://worldpopulationreview.com. Accessed June 6, 2022.

MacLean, V.; & Williams, J. (2005). Sociology at women's and Black colleges. In A. Blasi (Ed.), *Diverse histories of American sociology* (260–316). Leiden: Brill.

Marmot, M. (2004). *The status syndrome: how social standing affects our health and longevity.* New York: Henry Holt.

Mayo-Smith, R. (1895). *Statistics and sociology.* New York: Macmillan.

Mays, B.; & Nicholson, J. (1933/1969). *The Negro's church.* New York: Russell and Russell.

McRoberts, O. (2003). *Streets of glory: church and community in a Black urban neighborhood.* Chicago: University of Chicago Press.

Merton, R. (1938). Social structure and anomie. *American Sociological Review*, 3, 672–682.

Mills, C. (1959). *The sociological imagination.* New York: Oxford University Press.

Morris, A. (2007). Sociology of race and W. E. B. Du Bois: the path not taken. In C. Calhoun (Ed.), *Sociology in America: a history* (503–534). Chicago: University of Chicago Press.

Morris, A. (2015). *The scholar denied: W. E. B. Du Bois and the birth of modern sociology.* Oakland: University of California Press.

Murdock, G. (1949). *Social structure.* New York: Macmillan.

Myrdal, G. (1944). *An American dilemma: the Negro problem and modern democracy.* New York: Harper & Row.

Nelsen, H.; & Kanagy, C. (1993). Churched and unchurched Black Americans. In D. Roozen and C. Hadaway (Eds.), *Church & denominational growth* (311–323). Nashville: Abingdon Press.

Niebuhr, H. (1929). *The social sources of denominationalism.* New York: Holt.

Odum, H. (1951). *American sociology: the story of sociology in the United States through 1950.* New York: Longmans, Green.

Park, R.; & Burgess, E. (1921). *Introduction to the science of sociology.* Chicago: University of Chicago Press.

Park, R.; Burgess, E.; & McKenzie, R. (1925). *The city.* Chicago: University of Chicago Press.

Patterson, O. (2000). Taking culture seriously: a framework and Afro-American illustration. In L. Harrison and S. Huntington (Eds.), *Culture matters: how values shape human progress* (202–218). New York: Basic Books.

Perrin, N. (1969). *What is redaction criticism?* Philadelphia: Fortress Press.

Population of states and counties of the United States: 1970–1990. Lowndes County, Alabama. Population 2022. https://worldpopulationreview.com. Accessed March 14, 2022.

Portes, A. (1987). The social origins of the Cuban enclave economy of Miami. *Sociological Perspectives*, 30, 340–372.

Putnam, R. (2020). *Bowling alone: the collapse and revival of American community—revised and updated*. New York: Simon & Schuster Paperbacks.

Quinn, B.; Anderson, H.; Bradley, M.; Goetting, P.; & Shriver, P. (1982). *Churches and church membership in the United States 1980*. Atlanta: Glenmary Research Center.

Rabaka, R. (2010). *Against epistemic apartheid: W. E. B. Du Bois and the disciplinary decadence of sociology*. Lanham, MD: Lexington Books.

Rauschenbusch, W. (1907/2007). *Christianity and the social crisis in the 21st century*. P. Rauschenbusch (Ed.). New York: Harper One.

Reiss, I. (1988). *Family systems in America*. New York: Holt, Rinehart & Winston.

Riordan, C.; & Mazur, A. (1988). *Introductory sociology workbook*. New York: Harper & Row.

Roof, W. (1993). *A generation of seekers: the spiritual journeys of the baby boom generation*. San Francisco: Harper Collins.

Roof, W.; & Johnson, Sr., M. (1993). Baby boomers and the return to the churches. In D. Roozen and C. Hadaway (Eds.), *Churches & denominational growth* (293–310). Nashville: Abingdon Press.

Seccombe, K.; & Kornblum, W. (2020). *Social Problems* (16th ed.). New York: Pearson.

Small, A.; & Vincent, G. (1894) *Introduction to the study of society*. New York: American Book Company.

Stark, R. (1992). The reliability of historical United States census data on religion. *Sociological Analysis*, 53, 91–95.

Stark, R. (2004). *Exploring the religious life*. Baltimore: Johns Hopkins University Press.

Stark, R. (2007). *Sociology* (10th ed.). Belmont, CA: Cengage Learning.

Stark, R.; & Finke, R. (2002). Beyond church and sect: dynamics and stability in religious economies. In T. Jelen (Ed.), *Sacred markets, sacred canopies*, (31–62). Lanham, MD: Rowman & Littlefield.

Sumner, W. (1906). *Folkways: a study of the sociological importance of usages, manners, customs, mores, and morals*. Boston: Ginn.

Theissen, G. (2007). *Erleben und verhalten der ersten Christen: eine psychologie des Urchristentums*. Gutersloh: Gutersloher Verlagshaus.

Theissen, G.; Chan, C.; & Czachesz, I. (2017). *Kontraintuitivitat und paradoxie: zur kognitiven analyse urchristlichen glaubens*. Berlin-Munster: LIT Verlag.

United States Census Bureau. (1913). *1910 Census: Volume 2. Population reports by states, with statistics for counties, cities, and other civil divisions: Alabama–Montana*. www.census.gov/library/publications/1913/dec/vol-2-population.html.

United States Census Bureau. (2007). Population distribution by age, race, nativity and sex ratio, 1860–2005. www.census.gov and www.infoplease.com.

United States Census Bureau. (2020). Quick facts: Lowndes County, Alabama. Population Census 2020. www.census.gov/quickfacts/fact/table/lowndescountyalabama/PS7045221.

United States Department of Commerce and Labor. (1910). E. Dana Durand, Director. *Religious bodies:1906*. Part 1. Summary and General Tables. Washington, DC: U.S. Government Printing Office.

Unknown. (1900). *The Philadelphia Negro: a social study* by W. E. Burghardt Du Bois. *American Historical Review*, 6, 162–164.

Wallace, W. (1971). *The logic of science in sociology.* New York: Aldine de Gruyter.

Ward, L. (1883). *Dynamic sociology or applied social science as based upon statical sociology and less complex societies.* New York: E. Appleton. Second edition published in 1897.

Washington, B. (1901/2003). *Up from slavery.* New York: Barnes & Noble.

Washington, B.; & Du Bois, W. E. B. (1907). *The Negro in the South.* Philadelphia: George W. Jacobs.

Weber, M. (1904–1905, 1920/1996). *The Protestant ethic and the spirit of capitalism.* T. Parsons (Trans.) and introduction by R. Collins. Los Angeles: Roxbury.

Weber, M. (1922/1964). *The sociology of religion.* E. Fischoff (Trans.) and introduction by T. Parsons. Boston: Beacon Press.

White, L. (2010). *Scripting Jesus: the gospels in rewrite.* New York: Harper One.

Wilson, W. (1996). *When work disappears: the world of the new urban poor.* New York: Knopf.

Wilson, W. (2009). *More than just race: being black and poor in the inner city.* New York: W. W. Norton.

Wilson, W. (2012). *The truly disadvantaged: the inner-city, the underclass, and public policy* (3rd ed.). Chicago: University of Chicago Press.

Wilson, W.; & Taub, R. (2006). *There goes the neighborhood: racial, ethnic, and class tensions in four Chicago neighborhoods and their meaning for America.* New York: Alfred A. Knopf.

Wimberley, R.; & Morris, L. (1997). *The southern black belt: a national perspective.* Lexington, KY: TVA Rural Studies, University of Kentucky.

Wirth, L. (1938). Urbanism as a way of life. *American Journal of Sociology,* 44, 8–20.

Woolever, C.; & Bruce, D. (2010). *A field guide to U.S. congregations* (2nd. ed.). Louisville: Westminster John Knox Press.

Wortham, R. (2005a). Du Bois and the sociology of religion: rediscovering a founding figure. *Sociological Inquiry,* 75, 33–452.

Wortham, R. (2005b). An introduction to the sociology of W. E. B. Du Bois. *Sociation Today,* 3, 1, www.ncsociology.org/sociationtoday.

Wortham, R. (2005c). The early sociological legacy of W. E. B. Du Bois. In A. Blasi (Ed.), *Diverse histories of American sociology* (74–95). Leiden: E. J. Brill.

Wortham, R. (2009a). W. E. B. Du Bois, the Black church, and the sociological study of religion. *Sociological Spectrum,* 29, 144–172.

Wortham, R. (2009b). W. E. B. Du Bois and the scientific study of society: 1897–1914. In R. Wortham (Ed.), *W. E. B. Du Bois and the sociological imagination: a reader, 1897–1914* (1–20). Waco: Baylor University Press.

Wortham, R. (Ed.). (2018a). *W. E. B. Du Bois and the sociological study of the Black church and religion, 1897–1914.* Lanham, MD: Lexington Books.

Wortham, R. (2018b). Editor's introduction. In R. Wortham (Ed.), *W. E. B. Du Bois and the sociological study of the Black church and religion, 1897–1914* (1–22). Lanham, MD: Lexington Books.

Wright, C. (1900). *Outline of practical sociology: with special reference to American conditions.* New York: Longmans Green.

Wright, E., II. (2002a). Why Black people tend to shout! an earnest attempt to explain the social negation of the Atlanta Sociological Laboratory despite its possible unpleasantness. *Sociological Spectrum,* 22, 335–361.

Wright, E., II. (2002b). The Atlanta Sociological Laboratory 1896–1924: a historical account of the first American school of sociology. *Western Journal of Black Studies*, 26, 165–174.

Wright, E., II. (2006). W. E. B. Du Bois and the Atlanta University Studies on the Negro revisited. *Journal of African American Studies*, 9, 3–17.

Wright, E., II. (2008). Deferred legacy! The continued marginalization of the Atlanta Sociological Laboratory. *Social Compass*, 2, 195–207.

Wright, E., II. (2016). *W. E. B. Du Bois and the Atlanta sociological laboratory: the first American school of sociology*. Farnham, UK: Ashgate.

Wright, E., II; Calhoun, T. (2006). Jim Crow sociology: toward an understanding of the origin and principles of Black sociology via the Atlanta Sociological Laboratory. *Sociological Focus*, 39, 1–18.

Zamir, S. (1995). *Dark voices: W. E. B. Du Bois and American thought, 1888–1903*. Chicago: University of Chicago Press.

Zuckerman, P. (2002). The sociology of religion of W. E. B. Du Bois. *Sociology of Religion*, 63, 239–253.

Zuckerman, P. (2009). The irreligiosity of W. E. B. Du Bois. In E. Blum and J. Young (Eds.), *The souls of W. E. B. Du Bois* (3–17). Macon: Mercer University Press.

Zuckerman, P; Barnes, S; & Cady, D. (2003). The Negro church: an introduction. In W. E. B. Du Bois (Ed.), *The Negro church* (vii–xxvi). Walnut Creek, CA: AltaMira Press.

Index

About the Author

Robert A. Wortham is now retired from academia but was affiliated with North Carolina Central University for thirty-four years (1988–2022). Trained as an interdisciplinary scholar and teacher (PhD, Emory University), he served as a professor of sociology for twenty-five years and then served as an associate dean for two colleges and an interim dean for a total of nine years. He is the author of numerous articles on W. E. B. Du Bois and is the editor of four books on Du Bois' early sociological activities. His most recent edited book is *W. E. B. Du Bois and the Sociology of the Black Church and Religion, 1897–1914*, also published by Lexington Books.

www.ingramcontent.com/pod-product-compliance
Lightning Source LLC
Chambersburg PA
CBHW062034270326
41929CB00014B/2424